Money Train ...
Money Trap

Money Trail . . . Money Trap

How to Win in the Stock Market

DONALD COBBETT

With a Foreword by R. C. Beckman

Cartoons by

MERCURY BOOKS
Published by W.H. Allen & Co. Plc

First published in 1989
by the Mercury Books Division of
W.H. Allen & Co. Plc
Sekforde House, 175–9 St John Street, London EC1V 4LL

Set in Concorde by Phoenix Photosetting
Printed and bound in Great Britain by
Mackays of Chatham PLC, Chatham, Kent

British Library Cataloguing in Publication Data
Cobbett, Donald
Money trail – money trap.
1. Great Britain. Stock markets – For
investment
I. Title
332.64′241

ISBN 1–85252–031–0

CONTENTS

To my five grandsons –
Johnny, Marcus, Sam, Alexis and Gregory:
this will be the last subjection
to your grandfather's belief
in his literary prowess.
Oh, good!

ACKNOWLEDGEMENTS

Grateful thanks and acknowledgements to my confers, collaborators and correctionists (in so far as they might, in these ever-changing circumstances), for their invaluable help towards my swansong ... (Or the last was to be that, was it not, Nicholas Pine?)

Specially, I have to thank Bob Beckman, diverted from his, I know, insuperable labours, to pen me such a fulsome foreword. Then onwards, in turn, to the several financial scribes from whose work I have sought, with accompanying acknowledgements, supportive extracts for my views.

I have, in addition, to acknowledge John Murray (Publishers) Ltd for permission to quote 'The City' by John Betjeman. Also thanks to both Mr David Hopkinson and Mr Stanislas Yassukovich, for full transcripts of their views referred to in my Chapter 9, 'Climate of the Unstoppable'.

To those divers departments of the ISE, and including personally Stuart Valentine, of the Retail Marketing Unit; as also officers of the Department of Trade and Industry, thank you for responding to my inquiries.

Donald Cobbett
London, 1989

By the same author

TALES OF THE OLD STOCK EXCHANGE
BEFORE THE BIG BANG

To those who ask perplexedly, 'What was it like before this much heralded "Big Bang"?' . . . well, here it all is – amusing, instructive, pathetic, heroic – the stories great and small, the slumps and booms, the market by-play, here they all are . . .

Donald Cobbett, who incredibly spans lightly the succeeding decades with his anecdotal colloquial memories of Throgmorton Street, from humble 'blue button' clerk in the Great Slump to broker-member, financial writer, many times columnist, speaker on the practice and history of the market place, tells of:

- Some of the tricks and ruses played by dubious brokers to part clients from their money
- How jobbers really work – not, perhaps, how you might think
- Some of the jokes and jests played in the house and the finer points of dart throwing!
- What exactly the fiddles are that brokers can or did get up to
- Why tobacco shares were marked down on Gandhi's death
- The 'Tea and Tickle' shops – who would have thought it?
- How Branston Pickle got its name
- The bookies – how and where the full service ran on the very floor of the house

Price: £2.95 (paperback), 128 pages, 25 cartoons

Available by post direct from the publishers: Milestone Publications, 62 Murray Road, Horndean, Hants PO8 9JL

FOREWORD

by R. C. Beckman

Over the past few decades I've spent as a member of the investment industry, I've learned an amazing fact. Investors know practically nothing about how the investment industry works. But, I've also learned it's not their fault. The City likes it that way – and capitalises on it with complicated deals, confusing prospectuses, indecipherable nomenclature, coupled with a language of 'Newspeak' and 'Double-Think' that would put George Orwell to shame.

Legitimacy in the investment world is conferred by credentials in economics, finance, business administration or some other dry disciplines of the natural sciences, openly displayed by those employed in the grandiose City institutions. Experts abound. Yet, few who express strong opinions on the market place have demonstrably profited by them. I've often said, 'If you were given the opportunity to look at your personal adviser's investment record, you'd probably run a mile.' While the City embroiders itself with men in pin-striped suits, flaunting their calling cards from mahogany desks, it's all part of investment 'show biz'. While the City fathers – the bankers and the brokers – would like to give you the impression that they're offering you the prayer rug at the temple of investment, in the final analysis, all you wind up with is a set of knee pads for the world's biggest floating crap game. This is the reality. It is a reality that has been brought home with a vengeance in this book. It is a reality that every investor should be aware of before he picks up a telephone to talk to his stockbroker or investment adviser.

This is not going to be your financial adviser's favourite book. It documents the inherent conflict of interest that exists between stockbrokers, financial planners and their clients, a conflict that has been amplified through deregulation and 'Big Bang'. The book is highly critical of the 'Big Bang' philosophy. It attempts to expose the cynicism with which the small private investor has been lured into the market on the trail of privatisations; then largely trapped, left marooned by the vicious rise in stockbrokers' commissions and fees. The charges by which financial advisers are paid has created a temptation to recommend products and services that pay the higher remuneration to the seller rather than those that may provide the client with the greatest benefit. Since the commissions and fees on some products are ten to twenty times greater than those on alternative investments, the temptation is a powerful one. And, in many cases, the charges may also be invisible. There is no greater demonstration of this tendency than the enormous incentives offered by the UK government itself to the brokers and agents who place the privatisation issues in the hands of the public.

In my thirty years as a professional adviser, I've seen the account pages of elderly people whose life savings have been squandered on excessive trading and risky securities. I've witnessed the fine points of artful misrepresentation that encourage a client to purchase an investment. I've attended sales meetings at stockbrokerage firms in which product promoters lead off their presentation with: 'Well, the first thing I'm going to tell you about this product is what you will want to know: the commission credit is 6 per cent.' And, I've heard the professional advisers laugh in unanimity.

Investors at large should be eternally grateful to Donald Cobbett for this no-holds-barred exposé on the multifaceted inequities that have resulted from the Government's policy for a new-born Square Mile and the successive jockeyists (from Parkinson downwards) who have implemented this ill-conceived policy. Part of the book may frighten unsophisticated investors, and make them feel they'd be best off stashing their money in a mattress. Although that would probably be better than placing blind trust in a stockbroker, it's unnecessary. The book is not meant to frighten you. It's meant to prepare you for dealing with the reality of the investment world in which you live – and the vested interests that comprise that reality.

No doubt there will be many critics who disagree with the conclusions . . . or what they perceive to be the conclusions. Some may also disagree with certain generalisations that are made. But, no one can disagree with the facts that are presented, because Donald Cobbett has been there. I've been there too!

PREFACE

Punch commented jocularly on my last paperback about the old-time Stock Exchange that the author was not a 'self-effacive man'. Admitting this perception, might I mention that, never content to keep within my fold, I attempted here again a concept of the cover design, although it was in the end substituted by the present games board layout. I conceived, as explicit of my purpose in this book, the wet, ridged sand left by a retreating tide, with its shoals and pitfalls ... deceptively treacherous for the novice investor's first faltering footsteps into a beckoning stock market.

Having pointed the way with this basic idea, I must now stress that to write with any conviction on the practice of investment in this mercurial stock market, one should view the scene at long range. Too much water is cascading under the bridge to attempt the specifics.

It is the underlying principles of investment to which one must now devote oneself, not the procedure or what might be called, with literal truth, the 'mechanics'. Because everything now is resolved (an ambitious belief, come to think of it) by switch or press-button.

Indeed, any resemblance in the present electronically based dealing system to what we once knew as *The* Stock Exchange, and before that, more intimately, as just the Stock Exchange,

London, has disappeared totally and irretrievably. Frail façades, such as the Stock Exchange Investors' Club and the Visitors' Information Centre (erstwhile Gallery), have been erected and embellished in the pretence that there is still a public identity with the emblazoned crest (its once honoured boast, 'My Word is My Bond') on the wall of the historic Capel Court entrance.

But all this is no more reality than the memorial to some long dead dignitary beside a portico in Bloomsbury. It is questionable which means least to the break-neck professionals of today – the gilded legend or the mechanically turned pages of the roll of honour commemorating our dead of successive wars.

It is perhaps forgotten that even after the second, still temporary, removal of the mining market to the Tower Block improvisation, the old Rhodesian jobbers were still keeping the flag of independence literally flying in dogged support of Ian Smith's UDI . . . and, of all perversity, five years after the actual event. If the membership had shown the same determination in opposition to this Government's mistaken vision of a new professionalism, internationalism and competition in the Square Mile, we might not have been engulfed in the tears shed so profusely in under a year of the electronic miracle of Big Bang.

So now we have not *The* Stock Exchange, but *The International* Stock Exchange, in acknowledgement of the jostling foreign interests – banks, brokers, Down Under infiltrators, bingo-callers, jolly order-swappers – who have swamped our jealously guarded sanctum, stripped it of its high traditions, and left it in the hands of tiered bodies of regulators totally unaware of, and insensitive to, the past. The Stock Exchange Council's authority has been watered down by an influx of outsiders who, with respect, know little of the historic background of the market-place or of the intricacies of its old workings.

I have many times, in my writings, told of my sombre beginnings as a 'Blue Button' clerk in that lovely August of 1933; told of how the beginner is inevitably coloured by his first environment; of how I have always looked askance at the popularly supposed 'good time', and ignored (often at my cost) the confidential nudge to place my shirt on this or that.

The newcomer to the stock market setting forth on the money trail down the Street called Throgmorton – the Street reputedly paved with gold – is not short of glib guides to the gullible through the shoals and quicksands. Seemingly so many 'experts'. The letterbox is daily bombarded by well-wishers offering the proverbial pound for a shilling – or, nowadays, on the retrospective refrain of seven years of persistently rising share prices, £50,000 for £5,000. As a well-known entrepreneur friend of mind always gleefully shouted down the cold callers, 'Well, if it's so easy, why don't you do it yourself?'

The institutional advocates advertising in the better Sunday papers, expansive as the seedsmen's catalogues in spring, parade a grandiose range of goodies: income returns with minute asterisks, potential profit in everything from wines, woolly lambs, smoked salmon, to apples on the tree, the handling of his/her modest savings in every plausible shape and form. Each and every one of these persuaders is possessed of one idea – to get hold of the individual's laboriously earned or fortuitous savings, and garner them to a management account.

To whose account? This is the question to which the ambitious fingering their cheque-books must address themselves.

Yet the oft-cautioned newcomer will protest: So what? We've heard it all before. The booksellers' shelves are ranged, spine by spine, with good advice by Square Mile experts on the need to tread cautiously. Why, then, do so many still fall for the whispered word of wisdom from the horse's mouth?

A little tale now to underline the answer to this question. I well remember how in the summer of 1919, when I was coming eight, my late father, together with an uncle by marriage, a merchant naval officer no less, sailed an old ship's gig from Ramsgate to Broadstairs. Not a portentous maritime feat, on a brilliant August afternoon with a light breeze, a favourable tide, and a distance of perhaps three nautical miles of coastal waters.

The well-remembered *Rover* entered Broadstairs main bay, at extreme high water, with inconspicuous sailsmanship; the mainsail half down, boom trailing abeam; the occupants fallen over among the entanglement of gear; the boat luffing and bluffing on the sultry swell.

Viewing this spectacle with polite absorption was the holiday populace. My embarrassed mother was leaning on the jetty bulwark next to an aged bargee who, after a lengthy pause for reflection, slowly removed the sucked clay from his mouth and emitted this weighty comment: 'No words c'tell, no larning . . . .. 'tis only 'xperience.'

That's what I mean. Not only about stocks and shares and so much else. In all the welter of post-mortems I have read on the causes of the Black Monday débâcle, few stated, first and foremost, that if a minority was dishonest whether by neglect or with intent, the majority was woefully ignorant and inexperienced. If the Government, the Bank of England, the Department of Trade, all the practitioners and custodians of high propriety foisted on the Square Mile, had been really experienced, and not filchings from the cradle (why rely on these ridiculous head-hunters?), then things might have been kept in perspective and proper proportion.

Above all, this book aims at repairing a few of the glaring gaps in the experience field.

Donald Cobbett
LONDON, 1988

Money Trail . . .
Money Trap

The City

Businessmen with awkward hips
And dirty jokes upon their lips
And large behinds and jingling chains
And riddled teeth and riddling brains
And plump white fingers made to curl
Round some anaemic City girl,
And so lend colour to the lives
And old suspicions of their wives.

Young men who wear on office stools
The ties of minor public schools
Each learning how to be a sinner
And tell 'a good one' after dinner,
And so discover it is rather
Fun to go one more than father.
But father, son and clerk join up
To talk about the Football Cup.

John Betjeman

1

THE PSYCHOLOGY OF INVESTMENT

Because capital security is the first principle of sound investment, I stressed in my preface the defensive purpose of my advice. My underlying theme, at the same time, is the repetitive pattern of the stock market, and how without descending to complicated depths in the technique of chartism, the newcomer may learn profitably from a study of past performance. The simple truth is that because of the interplay of greed and fear, history slavishly repeats itself.

Put another way, this is my digest from sixty years' experience in and around Throgmorton Street of the 'psychology' of dealing (dignify it *investing*, if you will) in stocks and shares. But as my family would remark, deprecatingly, 'You know nothing about psychology, Donald.' True, but I have learned over the decades a deuce of a lot about what makes the market tick – and when.

Principles Not Procedure

I am concerned at the outset to make it abundantly clear that while the 'mechanics' and procedure of the market-place have been radically overturned since Big Bang, on 27 October

[3]

1986, yet the underlying principles of investment – particularly, say, the vital timing – are totally unchanged . . . and unchanging. For example, at rock bottom, your stock, share, house, car, antique, what you will, is only disposable on another's ability – and willingness – to buy. And vice versa. If there is no such dependence your valuables or necessities are temporarily worthless.

Secondly, no wondrous computer knows more than the present moment in time; it has no imaginative flair. And imagination is the keynote of successful investment. So quoth an old entrepreneurial friend of mine, who left his late-late-late Majesty's hospitality in the early 1930s and straightway booked in at the Ritz with a couple of bricks in his suitcase. Imagination.

But then, in his heyday of affluence, this gentleman had been well known to the doormen around the precincts of Piccadilly for his high-stepping horses. He always instructed me that so long as one could stride with the confidence of knowing precisely one's way along the thickly carpeted corridors of the most eminent establishments, one could relieve, wash and pomade oneself both comfortably and economically. A precept I have invariably followed with success. More imagination.

Accuracy of an Automaton

In these times of highly mechanised stockbroking, mega-deals via satellites and banks of electronics, it is a common fallacy among those who do not indulge in stocks and shares to suppose that those who do are enabled to perceive the market with the accuracy of an automaton.

This dangerous confidence is due in part to the new-style commentators and top salesmen. Brash without brilliance, they project what are now termed financial 'products': what we formerly called, in our lower key, stocks, shares, and trust units. Combined with these sages of the Square Mile are the modern journalists who continually defer with nauseating familiarity to every word they utter or pen.

Quoting at random from the paper at my side, I read (with names amended) . . . Alic Sliprule, analyst of broker Bumstrum, believes the current fall in Naughty Nighties provides an ideal buying opportunity . . . Bill Pickup, Proctor Pramble's marine surveyor's estimate of Limpet Lines, is for a downgrading of profits . . . So-and-so says or forecasts this, that, or miraculously the other. And it is all received with unquestioning reverence by the young scribes. Everybody's comments are, if possible, heavily personalised.

Missive from a Broom Cupboard

When I was a youngster on the Stock Exchange (no imperious *the* in those days), stockbrokers employed, at best, a background stats man who ventured a few guarded views for the aspiring client. Nobody then, save the bucket-shop proprietor, dared voice much hard advice . . . an opinion perhaps over a glass of fino sherry in Slaters, but little specific beyond a few lines of type contrived by a bewhiskered spinster in pebble glasses entombed in a species of broom cupboard.

Looking back into the cavernous decades, I can recall that, in accompanying my father in his forays to Throgmorton Street in the late 20s, our broker, a family friend, allayed many a statistical inexactitude with a glass of fino over the Street. As elsewhere at business, Mr Child wore his inseparable topper in the office, tipped jauntily to the back of his head. It was strictly City gear. When he departed of an afternoon, he parked it atop of the high, gaunt, iron safe, neatly enveloping

Dealing was done physically, eyeball to eyeball . . .

the milk bottle, as a gesture to hygiene. Oh, things were very different in those days!

Electronic Stampede

The important difference to today's electronic stampede by the professionals was that the dealing was done physically, eyeball to eyeball, the unshakeable verbal bargain, on the floor of the House. This is where a stock market speaker at an explanatory session I recently attended went slightly astray. He conceived the broker-member as repeatedly sending his dealer minion into the market to check, re-check, and finally to deal in the shares concerned. Not so. The broker would himself have assessed the price basis, personally relayed it to his client waiting in the 'Street', then dealt. The business was not, as nowadays, rigidly office-bound. Keen public operators gravitated to the 'Street'; the inveterate speculators, known as kerb-crawlers, regularly inhabited the pavements attended by their half-commission men.

Self-acclaimed Experts

In recent years the supplicant small investor, obeisant in the market-place, avid for the pearls of wisdom dropped from the tables of the self-acclaimed 'experts', has been paralleled by the advisers themselves – bank-inflated stockbrokers, market-makers (erstwhile jobbers), so-called counsellors (Heaven save the mark!), unit trust managers, building society moguls aspiring beyond their last, spell-binders and pedlars. Advisers all. Never perhaps since the South Sea Bubble were there so many and so ill-informed.

So, to the real advice. Remember this: if most of the documentation today comes clinically clean from shiny computers, it is still the heart, not the mechanism, that determines the market trend. Opinion makes the market and the inconsistency of the market is due to the fact that opinion is often far from critically based. It is widely swayed by the rival emotions of greed and fear, as I emphasised in the opening of this chapter. And the great deception lies in the fact that both are self-generating. Optimism proliferates with success; pessimism perpetuates failure. Which is precisely why the investor at large – not to mention many of the professionals – invariably misjudges the crucial turning points in the market's overall cycles.

Plateauing Phase

Successful investment, it follows, depends on some understanding of psychology. Indeed, charts and indices, on which so many religiously rely, are really an application of this technique to the interpretation of stock market trends. They depict, in figurative and diagrammatic form, progressions from which reasonable assumptions may be drawn as to future behaviour. What they show, in fact, is that human nature does not change; that an ascension of optimism over pessimism, or the reverse, is likely, other things equal, to be perpetuated into the future.

What happens in practice is that the investor at large becomes so persuaded by the inevitability of an established trend, so seduced by success or submerged by failure, that judgement is clouded and there is a failure to change step in sufficient time. Judgement can seldom have been more impenetrably clouded than in the early autumn of 1987.

For the reasons I have indicated, at the peak of the 'bull'

market, as in the trough of the 'bear', there is usually what I have described as a *plateauing* phase when the market either shades from the top or stirs off the bottom, to move, as we say, 'sideways' for a time within narrow bounds.

The reason for this plateauing is that, although the market is already reacting to fundamentally changing influences, the investor is obstinately buying against the trend or, conversely, jettisoning his shares on the least lift from the bottom. To the extent that the market normally moves in less dramatic fashion than recently witnessed, both in retreat from the peak and recovery off the bottom, underlying trends at these stages may be deceptively contradicted. At the same time it might be claimed that now, with the more violent and sporadic ups and downs, the real turning points in the primary trends are still more difficult to detect.

Swim with the Tide

The investor who employs a little psychology will appreciate, therefore, that there are times when it pays to swim conveniently with the tide, as equally there are others when it pays (and often far better) to go perversely counter to the popular trend. In the early stages of a recovery, by all means join the bandwagon and enjoy the propulsive power of the herd instinct as the popular appetite is whetted by easy profit. The art of astute timing lies in knowing when to disengage and encash one's investments. But to abandon the market when most others are assailing its final heights, when the stars seem so firmly set in the ascendant, is easier to advise than to act upon. Equally, it takes determination to commit capital when the bottom seems likely to fall out of the market.

In entering at the market's ebb, allow that your share selections may be continually redressed, in the early stages of revival, by disillusioned holders thankfully taking advantage of the first upturn to cut their losses. Until the pipeline is cleared of wreckage from the past, the result of injudicious purchases at the wrong prices (which is not to say fundamentally the wrong shares), recovery prospects will not blossom. It is only when a new generation of holders is firmly in the saddle that it is possible to sense the trends and feel the pace of the market.

Pursuing the psychological aspect, there is something to be learned, too, from the traditional pattern of the financial year. Recalling that most hackneyed of old market saws, 'Sell in May and go away', which has been as many times disproved as confirmed if you look back further than twenty years (to take one young journalist's time-span), there are several other milestones along the way worthy of acknowledgement.

Take, for another example, the fairly regular pre-Christmas euphoria, followed as regularly by New Year indigestion, both gastronomic and financial. During the mid-December phase everybody is insulated from financial reality by the festive distractions and prices pleasantly cocooned in tinsel. It is often worth selling into this mirage, because, three-to-one, January markets will fall on the fallow ground of bills and belly-ache. Do not lament at having missed your chance, however, as the Budget season will soon be beckoning and hopes will spring as they eternally do in the run-up to mid-March. But remember, in addition, that, more often than not, Budgets prove a wet squib.

If, indeed, you should have 'sold in May' and departed on holiday with the other malcontents, be sure to take your seat again by mid-August. September, with the return of the bronzed holiday-makers, is generally judged the time of re-kindled activity, but it is a further consideration that everybody is keen to beat the pistol. So mid-August will often see the first autumn stirring. But remember, with all this, the proviso: *other things equal.*

'Boot-strings' Business

The mistake made by most newcomers to the market-place is in believing that the vital turning points in the long, primary cycles are proclaimed by some clarion call, that there is a convenient revelation of some grand design for the way ahead. Rather does the investor have to strain for the tinkling of cymbals as the market mysteriously elevates itself by way of its own boot-strings. Those who wait impatiently on events may often wait in vain, because they will miss the subtle 'feel' of the market as sentiment shifts and confidence builds progressively from fragile beginnings.

Long familiarity with the stock market breeds an attitude of cynicism. One learns from experience that it tends to sow, in the seeds of its own prosperity, the harvest of its eventual undoing. On the other hand, and just as certainly, at the bottom of every slump lie the bare bones of the next boom. They only wait to be clad by the new circumstances from which will be argued fresh hopes for the future.

2

YOU, THE POPULAR INVESTOR

You are now, dear reader, in the age of the 'popular investor'. (You may choose to inflect the endearment to the monetary sense. Dear, indeed, for some, it may have proved!) For evidence of your proclaimed 'popularity', I would refer you to the successive initial issues of *Stockmarket*, the quarterly newsletter of the Stock Exchange Investors' Club first published in the early spring of 1987. In the opener, Sir Nicholas Goodison, then chairman of the ISE (The International Stock Exchange), espoused your cause:

> We have always supported the principle of wider share ownership. Direct investment in stocks and shares is not the preserve of the privileged few. It is available to everyone.

In the second issue, that of July, the Chancellor, Nigel Lawson, reinforced this with:

> This Government has always been firmly committed to extending individual share ownership. Policies such as privatisation and the encouragement of employee share ownership have contributed to a trebling of share ownership since 1979.

In unison, these two statements were emphatic enough, most would have thought. Combined with the blandishments with which the newcomer was cajoled into the ranks of the Government's long privatisation march, the appelate might

The encouragement of employee share ownership

be excused for having felt cosseted, embraced by the financial servicers offering the *choice* extolled by the Department of Trade and Industry, deserving of the attention and respect traditionally due to the customer . . . at least in England, whatever may be the attitude in America or Japan, far less in that hotbed of speculators Down Under.

Viewed in the light of experience over the past two years, the virtual underlining of the small investor's position expressed above can only be regarded, at best, as vastly over-optimistic. Because virtually in the wake of this enthronement, their 'popularity', correct as it might seem in numerical terms (9 million direct participants, it was reckoned), was far from being endorsed by the stockbroking community.

'An Introduction to the Stock Exchange'

I steadily gained the impression following the 19 October holocaust that the private investor was being treated, at best, with growing contempt; at worst, as non-existent. This despite authority's pious preaching of a popularity difficult to reconcile with the facts.

It is instructive to recall that, deferring to the ISE's own published guidance on its 'popular' servicers (*An Introduction to the Stock Exchange*, December 1987), Tony Blair, a Labour Party Treasury spokesman, in October 1987 condemned the cavalier treatment of the small, individual investor by a majority of stockbrokers/market-makers allegedly devoted, with solicitude, to the service of the little person.

According to Press reports at that time, he surveyed 151 firms, offering each a uniform selling order in 200 British Telecom. With one-third apparently declining to deal at all, his exercise threw up only thirty-six of the firms approached prepared to deal for a minimum commission of less than £20, plus VAT. Dated December 1988, a new, more cautiously worded, register of member firms prepared to undertake small investors' business, this time entitled the *Private Investors' Directory*, has been prepared by the ISE and is in circulation.

So much for 'popular' service. Since then a number of prominent stockbroking firms have purposely discarded the whole of their private clientele with little more than the drop of a circulated letter on the mat. Which was little short of telling them to pack off, lock, stock and barrel. The remedial recommendation in some such dismissals was in future to take their business to some suggested quarter.

Already, as I write this, two months ahead of implementation, the intended enforcement of a questionnaire (Letter of Agreement) on clients, attempting to extract intimate facts about financial ability (for instance, what credit cards do you use?), is being hotly criticised. Although, subject to The Securities Association's guidelines as to key points, the general form of their letter is left to the individual firm, dozens of stockbrokers, plus major banker-conglomerates, have recognised the consequences of attempting to probe into the affairs of long-established clients of proven solvency and total integrity. In some quarters literally hundreds of protests have been received. As one bank manager remarked, on being shown a rough of one such questionnaire, 'No way will they sign that!' As many of the questions to which answers are sought are grossly intrusive, I agree.

As a result of the reported dissension in the inner corridors of brokerdom, many are sending discreetly abridged letters and in divers forms to their established clients. To this extent, the imposition decreed – admittedly at third hand, looking first to Parliament – by the ISE's internally developed Self-Regulating Organisation (SRO), dubbed for this particular purpose The Securities Association (TSA), is hardly being fully implemented before it starts.

[15]

(This was roughly the position obtaining when I wrote the above last summer (1988). But, now, to placate the increasingly disenchanted private investor, the Securities Investment Board is modifying its insistence on 'Letters of Agreement' on the part of clients, and leaving a one-way passage in the matter of obligations and guidelines assumed and submitted by the stockbroker to his/her client. Apparently this is accepted as understood by the latter on a 'sign-and-return' basis. The SIB is insistent that, in the submitted statement of the broker's position and obligations, terms of dealing, there should be no individual provisos, nor any deviation from the original exact requirements. It seems to be that the onus for everything being in order will be squarely on the broker. I should add further that, in any case, for reason of necessary consultations, the final ruling will probably not be made before the spring. Should I be in error in my interpretation of what is in mind, then please substitute, elastically, the verb already used above – *modifying . . .*)

How many wheels within wheels, cogs and connivances, tiered meddlers, nannies and nobodies, there are in this multitudinous muddle and mismanagement called 'surveillance', I do not know. But I suspect this: they must together eventually stifle and snuff out the lingering flame of independent private business we once transacted in what was affectionately known as the 'House', but which is now supplanted by impersonal electronic display panels. To these, in mortal fear of retribution, the operators (your beleagured stockbroker or formerly obliging associate member) must slavishly defer.

Can the reader conceive of the tension imposed in the execution of a succession of orders each requiring the logging of possibly a dozen different details in a bargain record book? Since there are, even on the lamentably reduced business as I write, an average of nearly 21,500 general client 'trades' ('bargains' in old terminology) per session in UK equities – at least, there were in the end-September '88 quarter – you can imagine the extra paperwork, the added time in completing each instruction, particularly in the event of an avalanche of selling. Little wonder that the new protectionism is impeding the ready flow of business, and likely, I suggest, to clog the work considerably more when the requirements of the Financial Services Act are totally fulfilled. But not perhaps for the big institutional business which, because of its profitability, invariably edges to the front. The average volume turnover figure above, I should add, excludes a possible extra 3,961 trades per day between the market-makers themselves.

A Laconic Jargon

When I was a young man in the market-place, we exchanged some laconic jargon verbally with an opposite number, jotting the bargain details down in a penny notebook; from this the contract clerk meticulously inscribed the contract note in copperplate when the dealing books were handed in at 3.45 of an afternoon.

The other possible criticism of so-called 'Letters of Agreement' is that the Government has only recently decreed, in part contradiction of the above, that there should be careful control in the assembly and storage of credit control information. The public at large strongly object to the probing and prying into personal, particularly financial, details capable of being misrepresented or used injudiciously. And the individual now has the right, with reservations, to challenge the accuracy of such information. Whatever the assurances of confidentiality, we know only too well of the leakages from even the highest security quarters.

The further logical point is that, if the stockbroker claims the right of access to the affairs of his client, why equally should the client not have the right of access to all the relevant facts about his stockbroker? Quite clearly from recent happenings he/she has been far from favoured in this respect. It will be claimed that the current exchange of information already grants this mutual insight, but some of this charade is a cover-up for the fact that the widely cast net for new investors has regrettably enmeshed welshers too numerous for comfort. Many stockbrokers have admitted to me that they are continually being taken for the proverbial 'ride' and are scared of accepting newcomers.

Mutual Protection

To retreat five decades, I notice that one of the referral bodies from which information may be sought/checked about intended clients is still the old-established Stockbrokers' Mutual Reference Society. I can claim to know more than most about the Mutual Reference, because the firm of brokers with whom I sought sanctuary in 1935, after brief dalliance with the Dancing Doll (*Before the Big Bang*, p. 57), had as its senior partner the portly A. H. Glazier, who was additionally chairman of the said organisation in 1939–42. They nicknamed him, with penetrating aptitude, the Sussex Pig.

Further, the charming and efficient Miss N. H. Sutherland served for many of my years as manager of the MR, and had deeper roots in that she was the grand-niece of the Society's founder. The Mutual Reference was always traditionally hush-hush, distinctly in-house, so far as the public were concerned. It was instinctively suspected of keeping a 'black book' of recalcitrant payers: and so it did. Unfortunately in olden days insufficient resort was made to its services. But eventually it became obligatory to 'put' new clients through the screen. Sometimes Miss Sutherland would rummage among sheaves of dusty newspaper cuttings, with steadily falling countenance.

'You haven't dealt for him already, I hope, Donald?' she would inquire, looking up. I would confess uncomfortably that I had. It seemed that the miscreant had done everything short of a spell in gaol.

Doubtless this referral system has now progressed far beyond the dusty cuttings, is computerised and, as with everything else mechanical, is infinitely less amusing . . . even possibily efficient. I can more and more appreciate my friend John Smith's comment, when we bumped into one another in Bartholomew Lane back in 1984: 'You wouldn't like it now, Donald. It's not fun any more. They want you to justify yourself.' I knew what he meant. Justify myself is about the last thing I ever wanted to do!

Last Nails in the Coffin

The last nails are now being driven into the empty husk of Throgmorton Street, and maybe much else in the almighty City, by the stultifying strictures of 'surveillance', under the decrees of the Financial Services Act. And if it wasn't so sad it would be hilarious, because the victims, both stockbrokers and their 'popular' clients, are having to pay for the privilege of cutting their own throats.

As a director of the Stock Exchange Foreign Equity Market stated some time back, despite the inhibiting losses of the October crash, it would be forced to spend a suggested extra £50 million on new systems. Sir Nicholas Goodison, then chairman of the ISE's Council, remarked at about the same time that the cost of investor legislation conceived as protective would be passed on to that investor in dealing charges too high . . . 'for his survival', Sir Nicholas might have added. Everywhere now there is evidence that this is abundantly true: prominent stockbrokers are imposing a variety of basic annual fees, in addition to increased commission rates, for the maintenance of portfolios beyond just 'no frills' dealing. Even the most basic dealing commissions are going up everywhere, even as I write, by possibly 20%. And as the practitioners absorb, more and more, the costs of complying with the complex rules brought into existence by the Act, the more broker and client will become enmeshed in a vicious circle; the former battening down the hatches against ever rising cost and diminishing turnover, the latter, in horror at the frenzied efforts to recoup, abandoning the sinking ship. The straw of a new 80p levy on all equity bargains above £1,000 consideration has now been laid on the already restless camel's back. This is divided, fifty-fifty, between the Securities and Investment Board and the now subordinate Panel on Takeovers and Mergers. But this levy, too, has since come under review and may be amended or dropped.

Indirect Investment

In the area of what is known as 'family money', higher charges are, as I write (and I referred in my preface to the rapidity of the water under the bridge), seeping down from the direct to the indirect investor. Unit trusts were recently being cited as the first line of retreat behind the individual share purchase, but now, here again, the managements are tightening up their charges from the old ¾–1% to possibly 1.5%, reflective of surveillance costs. One large management group spoke to me of an extra burden of conceivably 'millions'.

It should be made clear that the management costs of running a unit trust fund are derived, firstly, from an initial charge of about 5% built into the offer price of the units. This is a one-off. Secondly, out of the dividend income accruing to the particular fund, there is an annual percentage accretion determined by the trust deed. The key point here is that if this rate of deduction is increased, it may be in mitigation of the gross income return. On some specifically growth funds the yields are already microscopic, and could, with permissible increases, be eliminated altogether. There is not the slightest doubt, from questioning around, that this continuing source of unit trust revenue will be increased (possibly by ¼–½%), and that attempts will be made to amend many of the now out-dated trust deeds to this end. These increases, both already imposed and in prospect, reflect the immense weight of the surveillance burden.

Since, at the same time, the scope for trusts generally gaining from 30–40% annually would seem to have been decimated by the sluggish performance of world stock markets, it is now hard to visualise the movement as the ideal alternative for the small person being encouraged to participate at secondhand.

To where will the poor 'popular' investor then retreat? And a still more pertinent thought: if the small investor should vacate this indirect form of share investment, what then of the trusts' main management income, on falling turnover, from the initial 'one-off' charge? It will sharply decline. I put this to one of the most reputable unit trust groups in the country, and the lady's most unequivocal reply was . . . 'Yes, that's right!' This fact apart from the underlying query as to how the managements will extricate dis-investors on the back of reluctant market-makers, and behind them (a devout hope), their much coveted institutions.

Partially in support of my views above, I quote instructively from a current Sunday newspaper, whose financial advertising is largely based on the exaltations and acclamations of the unit trusts . . . '[Their] net new investment . . . is down to a quarter of the levels enjoyed this time last year.' This was a comparison with April 1987. Further . . . 'Some unit trusts with £500 million or less under management are thought to be struggling to show much profit while new business continues at these levels.' It had been pointed out that gross sales up until then in 1988 were running some one-third down on the previous year. The combined effects of heavy encashments, diminished sales, and reduced opportunities for spectacular investment will be, as I emphasised above, seriously detrimental to management income.

Of all the recent privatisation issues, that of British Telecom in 1984, described by Bob Beckman as 'the archetypal People's Share', was reckoned to have increased the number of British shareholders by around 50%, to 3 million. Excellent as these shares may appear statistically as I write (250p compared with the full allotment price of 150p), Tony Blair's experience in the attempted disposal of 200-share lots around the market men was instructive of the degree to which the small investor may so easily become locked-in. And that in a leading equity. Mr Blair, incidentally, was at that time Labour spokesman for Treasury and Economic Affairs.

Problems of the Minor Equities

But what, then, of the out-of-the-way shares? Those to which I refer are the questionably liquid (some might claim, illiquid) delta securities, totalling, in representation of the UK and Irish markets, 414 in specific categories. Of these, 132 are currently equities. But remember that the constituent numbers, and necessarily then the total, are constantly changing. All these delta securities are outside the SEAQ (Stock Exchange Automated Quotations) system, but are listed in alphabetic order on TOPIC, which is the market's own information service. Market-makers are not obliged to quote prices on screen, but it is obligatory on them to make a two-way price in at least 100 shares over the telephone. The

Stock Exchange has now introduced a delta 'noticeboard' on TOPIC, advertising, on a bid and offer basis, such securities in this category in which it is wished to trade.

I should explain here that, in descending order of liquidity, the four categories in which the UK/Irish equities are dealt in on the ISE, with their current numbers, are:

$$
\begin{array}{lr}
\text{Alpha} & -\quad 136 \\
\text{Beta} & -\quad 595 \\
\text{Gamma} & -\ 1,754 \\
\text{Delta} & -\underline{\quad 132} \\
& 2,617
\end{array}
$$

Beyond these equity groupings there are related preference shares and all manner of prior charges (debentures, loan stocks, etc., most dated, a few totally undated), to an extent in excess of certainly 2,000. About the real marketability of these there is some elasticity, and the degree of their liquidity is the subject, as I write, of research. The market-makers do, I am told, run 'books' catering for most loan and preference capital issues, although not invariably on an instant two-way dealing basis.

It is most important, particularly from the point of view of executors left in impossibly trapped positions in winding up deceased accounts, that gamma and delta stocks and shares, particularly holdings in small and broken numbers, should be afforded a viable market. The point here is that holders from the past were publicly invited to subscribe their savings to issued (offered) share capital on the distinct understanding that the Stock Exchange (the institution under the old wholly elected internal Council) would ensure the maintenance of an adequate two-way market. This trust must be underwritten by the newcomers to the London market.

Question of Choice

I wrote (it was in mid-'85), and I still firmly believe, that whatever the claims about greater *choice* and competitive dealing costs for the small investor, the Government's Big Bang concept for the City would emasculate the former reasonably free market in small-priced, minor industrials. With the incursion of the mammoth marauders from overseas, not least the Americans, operators with not the slightest sensitivity about the past and its conditions for our people, this exclusion of the small investor from former dealing facilities was bound to happen, in the nature of human greed.

In the views I then expressed, referring in part to the alienation of certain issues, I wrote, in particular, fair and square:

> ... the strong will grow stronger, and the weak markedly more debilitated. The institutions ... now have the ball wholly in their court. Of the future, the danger ... visualised for the mass of investors, is of a two-tier, perhaps even a three-tier, market. An adequate market perhaps in 200/300 of the top equities; but an extremely questionable, perhaps wholly one-way, ultimately nonexistent, market in several thousand capital issues for the rest of us ... the Government, through the agency of its lackeys, talks blandly about the advantages of choice! I ask ... what choice for the small individual other than to invest at second hand via the vast collecting agencies for the public's savings?

... And so it has turned out.

In the event, prophetic, you'll think. Not at all: I know the Stock Exchange and its inner adherents, the base moneybags, too well. In every crisis of the past, for over half a century, I have watched with a wry smile of contempt the controlling partners jockey for the best available cover with total abandon. Looking back over my archives, I am amused to note that the Department of Trade and Industry thought my pre-Bang view of the market prospects seemed 'pessimistic'. I hardly think that could be agreed today.

A Viable Market

Traditionally, the stock market is thought of as both a *primary* and a *secondary* market. A primary market to the extent that new funds are raised from the investing public by way of the issue of new securities; a secondary market, in that trade takes place there in already established securities.

Of course, the two markets are inter-related, in that the willingness of investors to subscribe new capital in the primary market is critically dependent on their ability to dispose of such securities, if and when necessary, in the secondary market before their final maturity date. Some securities, such as ordinary shares and undated Government stocks, have no guaranteed maturity date. Hence the importance of preserving a viable market in perpetuity.

Put more directly (and here is the nub), if the investor had no confidence in his/her ability to encash their bits of paper (share certificates), they would never again put down their hard cash. You can only fool some of the people some of the time . . . !

What I have written above is perhaps the hard core of this book's title. The newcomer can easily be led out along the money trail, but once involved with even the most statistically attractive shares, how easy really is it to get out? This potentially is the money trap. So, if it is not a prime principle, as with security in the first chapter, it is very important nowadays to confine one's activities to the very, or at least reasonably, marketable shares – those in the alpha and beta categories.

3

FIRST FOOTSTEPS

Courses, books, lectures, lessons . . . almost everything explanatory on the subject of stock and share investment, all touch at an early stage on the necessity, as with the Canadian Mountie, of first 'getting your man'. By which is meant, in this context, making contact with a reliable, responsive, solicitous man of affairs – a stockbroker or his minion, the latter now tending to be known, in whatever capacity, as an 'employee'. All of which, of course, is extremely optimistic these days. Not least because the 'employee' is not necessarily salaried. It seems like one of those analogical descriptions often used in professional quarters to weave round something distasteful.

The Communicative Channel

The difficulty today in opening up a communicative channel to the market-place is that, whereas the aspiring client once had to seek out an aloof stockbroker by a process of formal introduction (say, via an accountant or solicitor), now the boot is somewhat on the other foot . . . the avid broker is more in pursuit, in so far as his straitjacket of regulations allows, of the perhaps elusive client.

The avid broker is more in pursuit

These days the stockbroker directly advertises his services, which would never, never have been allowed thirty years ago. Before the last war, and well into the peace, it was the jobbers who produced, and circulated from their pitches, the informative digests of company figures. You went to the leading jobber in, say, EMI and asked for a market 'slip'. These were printed as one, two and four-page folders identifiable as to source by the particular jobber's name. This was carried on a perforated tear-off strip, so that on dispatch to an inquiring client the anonymity of the publisher was preserved. At least, that was the charade.

In the light of today's hair-raising headlines, not only about the shortcomings of the leading miscreants, but behind these the lamentable counselling of intermediate (so-called) advisers, and therefore much awareness of the covetous eyes on his wallet, the pursued may be correspondingly the more wary, and the pursuer the more persistent. It is not merely a question of many market-makers throwing their private clients out with the bath water, but whether these too hasty gentleman will in future be able to hold what they deem their 'economic' business.

These several points raise my old fear that the new surveillance could be dangerously self-defeating. It is scandalous, I think, that the new enforced white surplice and diligently sucked peppermint should be looked for from the good, bad and indifferent, irrespective of background and former experience. In my earlier paperback, criticising the upheaval of the old market system, I particularly stressed the argument that the despised minimum commissions were a 'deterrent to reckless, and conceivably weak, under-cutters among brokers . . .'. This is one instance of how over-protection of the investor might lead in time, and quite legally, to practitioners over-baiting the hook to attract diminishing business. As with offers of too grandiose income returns, ultra-cheap dealing terms could well prove extremely expensive.

A great deal of advertising space is expended in the lure of the investor by all financial servicers, and such appeals will in future have to be extremely circumspect both in approach and phraseology. Now, too, that 'cold' (totally unsolicited) telephone calling and also unsolicited letters have been outlawed, the pressures on the private investor will be applied by more subtle means or at least with greater insistence.

The 'Popular' Investor Accepted as a Concession

Plagiarizing my own efforts from the past, I have referred continually to the rolled-out carpet, the silk-hatted partners genuflecting to their clients in the 'Street'; to fino sherry in Slaters, and the colloquial 'six-pounds-five', being the coveted penny-ha'penny commission on 1,000 shares.

But these are all of the past, consigned to a history multi-coloured by my own memories. Today the best the investor can look for is allocation to one of the chosen firm's associated members and subjection to a range of charges over and above basic commission, plus the requirement of an average bargain size of, at a minimum, £1,000.

Now the 'popular' investor is accepted, if at all, as a concession to the latter rather than as a privilege sought by the broker.

Pin-sticking

The old convention of making initial contact in the marketplace was, and still in part remains, a request to the International Stock Exchange, London, EC2N, for a short list of member-firms prepared to cater for a small investor.

Confronted impersonally by a list of mere names, it is hard to decide where one's interests are most likely to be best served. In some confusion about office addresses ranging from Palatial Buildings to Swill Alley and Chance Lane, the recipient finally sticks in several exploratory pins, writes off his requirements, and waits to be most amiably received – on paper – in the luck of his draw. He will probably receive a copy of the firm's latest circular and almost inevitably a 'private customer document', detailing with exactitude the terms on which your chosen firm would be prepared to act; also, for your signature, the contentious 'client registration form and financial questionnaire'.

Alternatively, an equally random choice may be made from the extensive list of acquiescent stockbrokers on pages 29–44 of the Stock Exchange's shiny booklet *An Introduction to the Stock Exchange*, now, as I have stated, substituted by a more subdued directory. However, the purely mechanical process of buying and selling can be effected equally well, and certainly with the maximum security for the client, by dealing directly through a bank. But it does help to have that little extra personal touch, the benefit of an occasional phone call or letter, somebody who may well become in time as much a confidant as a business adviser.

Apart from that, the actual dealing is likely to be done rather more painstakingly by going direct than by going through the bank channel, where your faceless order is formally processed through the mill with the rest of the particular bank's business. The added advantage of dealing through a stockbroker is that, in these days of precarious postal deliveries, contract notes and other documents could come to hand rather more quickly than in the case of working through a bank. Which leaves it to be conceded, somewhat contradictorily, that some banks will now deal with the immediate provision of a contract note, plus spot cheque or account credit in the case of a sale, provided they are accompanied by the relevant certificate.

The National Westminster has, as I write, over 250 branches affording virtually instant dealing in a wide range of leading equities. It is best, but not essential, to be a bank customer, and, in the case of being a purchaser, naturally to be in possession of the necessary outlay proposed. Other High Street banks have their own systems for readily dealing in shares.

Either way, banker or broker, the initiative is claimed nowadays to rest largely with the investor, who has continually, since Big Bang cast ethics to the winds, been advised to search diligently among the clamorous competitors. He/she has been enjoined to weigh carefully the services and charges offered in response to a written approach, telephone around at the prohibitive cost of peak hours, and make the coveted *choice* which the old Rule Book apparently denied. But I do not think so. You now have an illusory choice.

The Poor Man's Friend

I have repeatedly used the adjective 'small' for the investor with whom I am concerned. Like Pilate with his query on the ambiguous 'truth', what, in this context, is 'small'? The answer depends on the size and conception of the individual broker. In the upper echelons a portfolio of £100,000 might be regarded as small, if acceptable; but the poor man's friend could well be content to handle £5,000. With an employable capital of less than £5,000, however, direct investment is not cost-effective for either client or broker, and the prudent resort must be to some form of indirect investment. But with the present parallel rise in expenses, plus contracting revenue of the unit trusts, this, in turn, could be a somewhat tenuous route.

Before having achieved this new-found relationship with

an unexpectedly discovered stockbroker's attaché maybe two doors down in the same street, there is operationally the little matter of wherewithal . . . money, if you want the mundane. This may have accrued laboriously by hard work and prudent saving, or fortuitously by way of Aunt Matilda's little legacy, a lucky turn-up on the Premium Bonds, or some other unlikely coup. Should you be tempted, speculatively, to eye your cash-till in the High Street . . . don't! Final injunction: speculation, unless it might be forgotten, is at the risk of your wife's house-keeping; gambling, at the risk of your neighbouring wife's. The first is ill-advised; the second, suicidal. Never be a rapa-cious rifler of the magpie's nest.

Whatever the source, many beneficiaries or replete savers are consumed by the urge to do something right away, to the extent of sticking a pin in the share price columns of their newspaper. Anxious as they may be to consummate a new-found relationship with the market, and become for the first time recipient of a contract note, their agent, if playing straight by the new rules (and there is enough hot breath going down the collective neck to deter deflectors from the straight and narrow), will advise the newcomer strongly to resist any sense of urgency. As Bob Beckman concluded so amusingly and emphatically in his last book, *Into the Upwave*: 'Don't just *do* something – stand there!'

That, too, would be my inclination.

. . . And to the Cost Thereof!

Apart from the foreplay – the pin-sticking, the emergence of the amiable Mr Angles – your quest for the obliging stock-broker will be determined to a great extent by your assessment of the economics of the sheer dealing. Whatever the paragon in broker's surplice, sucking the aforesaid peppermint, you will be swayed by a parallel concern to deal through the least costly channel. But bearing in mind that the cheapest is seldom necessarily the best, let it be admitted at this point that we are now in a three-tier expenses system.

On the lowest scale, there is what is known as 'agency' dealing ... the basic, no-frills, straight trade on your own say-so, just what you instruct, buy/sell, so many, at hopefully so much. This is, as near as dammit, 'Do-It-Yourself'. Which the average person perversely prefers. It's more fun. I heard Harvey Jones, late of ICI, endorsing this same obvious view only recently on the radio. So those stockbrokers who cherish the idea of weaning the small person away into the weird and wonderful of their own in-house packaged concepts, do think again. For any affront to professional opinion by doing your own thing, you might get a glassy look, but conceivably do just as well – or better.

For this class of no-frills dealing, you will receive a confirmatory contract note within at least two days, and pay a commission of anything between £15 and £25. For the private person who wants to do his/her thing, this is the answer ... just a telephone order to the dealer assigned you, for execution at a pre-determined price – or 'at best'. Generally if it is right to deal, *deal*, and don't tie your man down too hard. That is a good old market maxim: in fact, deal when you can.

Next stage up, with more advice and exactitude, is what is termed the 'discretionary' service – meaning that the broker will consult you about your investment purpose, financial resources, needs. On the basis of a medium-sized portfolio (say, £50,000), your agency-broker will advise on appropriate action, timing, initiate switching where necessary, plus the documentation and background accounting. The last service might include for both security and convenience the registration of purchases in a nominee name. But all this with reasonable reference to the client. Because of the provision of concrete guidance, dealing charges for an advisory service like this will probably range between £20 and £30 per bargain, but much will depend on the consideration money in each case. With this approach, incidentally, the investor should go carefully into the terms of reference, particularly in respect of shared responsibility and access of portfolio checking.

Then, finally, there is the 'portfolio advisory' service, or call it full management. Again, in this case, it is essential to agree on the objectives right at the outset. It is the most suitable service for those who are fully occupied with business affairs elsewhere, and who would prefer an expert to determine policy, take over decisions, and do all the practical work in running their investment portfolios. This is the type of service, too, most suitable for expatriates. Stock purchased would be held for the client in safe custody in a nominee name, and the capital deployed subject to some surveillance by the client as described above. Again, charges per bargain will be on the high side, together perhaps with a small percentage calculated annually on the overall portfolio value.

Going to the 'Country'

A few words might be entered here about the possible advantages of dealing through, as we would have described it in the past, a 'country' stockbroker or 'countryman'. Because of the lower costs both in rentals and labour, those established in the big provincial cities and towns, not forgetting representation in the smaller, will frequently offer cheaper terms and a more personal service. So long as investors make abundantly sure that they are dealing with broker-members of the International Stock Exchange, then they are all linked in on the same computer network and are equally well vetted and regulated. Moreover, so far as local industries and firms are concerned, they are likely to be more intimately informed than their London competitors. So look about, and most conveniently, for brokers in your local area. You will probably not, in fact, have to look too far.

A further word about commissions and overriding charges. It is already visualised that supervision of a considerable sum, say, £100,000 upwards, will nowadays incur a supplementary fee in addition to commission on individual bargains. Some, as I write, are already charging £100 a year where accounts involve records and the preparation of valuations. On a portfolio of £100,000 this is modestly only 0.1%. At the same time, many investors are going to query whether agency-brokers can, in fact, justify such overriders in times of diminishing opportunity. Brokers, they will say, are quite willing to beat their own drum of adversity, but the squeezed client, in the vast majority, what of him?

Sugary Simplicity of the Merger-mongers

In an end-April (1988) article by financial journalist and former stockbroker Simon Rose, commenting on the discomfiture and increasing costs being suffered by stockbrokers in complying with the now 'voluminous rule books' imposed by the Financial Services Act, one is quoted as remarking:

> What is so annoying is that we now face increased costs to pay for the sins of others. The Stock Exchange has had a very good record of protecting investors over the years. The investment scandals have all occurred outside the Stock Exchange, usually fringe money advisers who have gone bust, who have absolutely nothing to do with you.

(*How very true in the light of the Barlow Clowes affair, dominating the headlines as I write.*)

The above extract precisely underlines what I earlier wrote myself about everybody unjustly being tarred with the same brush of suspicion. Whatever the arguments one side or the other, there is no question that, as love flies out of the proverbial window, the stockbroking community will be forced to close ranks still further by way of more mergers, and that the more monopolistic the profession becomes, the more progressively higher dealing costs will be hoisted.

Always I will remember, looking back over the years, the sugary simplicity of those circulated letters announcing market get-togethers . . . 'this amalgamation with our friends Caster and Runaway will, we are convinced, greatly heighten the level of services we are able to offer you, immensely strengthen the financial structure of our combined firms . . .' Not a word of truth in it. What was meant by the collective partners was that clients would hopefully fare the same, but that they themselves would stand to be bettered by way of a more substantial capital base, netting a double catch of clients under the one roof, with expenses substantially cut by the dismissal of redundant staff. Fine for the insiders, and the reason why they have latched on so eagerly to the widespread bank and institutional fusions. But, in the majority of cases, how mistakenly.

4

MONEY AND METHOD

Investment, fairly obviously, involves both money and method. The first it is now assumed we have. The means and costs of physically dealing in the market-place we have discussed, if with reservations. The more daunting next hurdle is how to deploy the money, in precisely what, and still more important, when? Alternatively, perhaps, there is the greater prudence of not deploying it at all. Indeed, brokers are now arguing the case for compensation for cautiously not dealing. 'Why,' say they, 'should we be penalised on this account?' Hence, as earlier mentioned, the looming overall percentage charge for portfolio supervision.

Mutual Understanding

In the tender beginnings, the first essential, on both sides, is a thorough understanding of the newcomer's financial resources and requirements (whether the emphasis is to be on capital growth or income?); then knowledge, recognition of the need for experienced guidance, and thus a reliable, communicative intermediary. This is a sort of restatement of The Securities Association's (TSA's) policy. It is precisely because of the abysmal lack of financial background, knowledge and experience that the authorities are so insistent on a clear definition of the guidelines on both sides. Even if the choice of investments is conceivably right, a lot depends, at the same time, on the prompt execution and reporting of orders, together with accurate processing and documentation.

So, in Turn, to the Method . . .

But before we consider in any detail how to invest in stocks and shares, it is essential, first, to grasp a few of the factors normally underlying market trends and thereby determining decisions. These I shall deliberately over-simplify, because, as is the case at the moment of writing, they are frequently falsified; and there are, besides, many interwoven facets and influences only confusing to the reader at an elementary stage.

Fundamentals of the Business

To delve now into a few of the fundamentals of the business. For example . . .

Investment decisions cannot be separated from the state of the world economy, and in particular the country in which the investments are based. If fixed-interest bonds (largely known here as 'gilt-edged' securities) are purchased just before a rise in the level of internal interest rates, investors will suffer a capital loss. The 'gilts' market is sensitive to inflationary pressures in the economy, and prices tend to rise when inflation appears to be falling and vice versa. Witness, as an instance, the over 74 points surge in Wall Street's Dow Jones industrial average, 31 May 1988, on allayed fears of a hoist in the US discount rate. On the following day the Dow plussed another 33 points.

Similarly, the purchase of ordinary shares (equities) just before a large downward movement in the market (e.g. the October 1987 crash) will make the investors wish they had purchased cash investments, contenting themselves with secure income. Thus the monitoring of economic conditions and successful investment must go hand-in-hand.

Academically, Not Always Practically

Hopefully this will prompt the reader to the conclusion that academically, which is not to say always practically, the main-spring of critical investment is the availability, and thereby the cost, of money itself. The nowadays base interest rate, substituted for the earlier Minimum Lending Rate, before that the old Bank Rate, is the most direct, but by no means the only, regulator by which the Government, via the Treasury and the Bank of England, seeks to spur or subdue the national economy. It is to this rate that our High Street banks conform, albeit at an interval, with all the other financial servicers in train, determining their lending and borrowing terms for the public.

What, then, does the cost of money – or, as the more technical put it, the level of interest rates – mean directly for the stock market? At its simplest, a cheap and plentiful money supply should (and I write 'should' advisedly, under these perverse conditions) equal a stimulated consumer demand, expanding trade, and a parallel confident, often buoyant, stock market. Conversely, a dear and curtailed money supply, such as suffered during the late 70s, is restrictive of consumer demand and business enterprise, and consequently depressive for the Stock Exchange.

'Gilts' the Pivot

For the stock market, Government (popularly known as 'gilt-edged') stocks constitute the pivot, by way of the interest rate. When this is high, in defence of the currency because there is the need to bait the hook more generously to attract foreign support for sterling, big money – indeed, all sorts of money – browses contentedly, if unexcitedly, in the safety-first pastures; it goes into depositories such as building societies and bank deposit accounts, and is loaned out to corporations where it is not subject to fluctuations and interest is correspondingly high. Investors stay rigidly on the sidelines.

With interest rates high, reflective of an adverse balance of foreign trade, and a consequent drain on the gold and currency reserves, the gilt-edged market falls both on uncertainty and the competition from still safer retreats; industrial ordinary shares conform in due turn to the diminished prospects.

But, on the contrary, when interest rates fall, reflective of improving trade and reviving confidence, then money is prompted out of its havens, first into gilt-edged and fixed-interest securities to secure the more tempting returns uncovered by their retreat, then progressively into a steadily widening field of ordinary shares as the prospects of reward are judged to outweigh the risks of loss.

'Capitalising Their Opportunities'

As with all factors motivating markets of whatever kind, the money supply, scarce or abundant, is self-generating either way. When credit is made more readily available, businessmen and investors alike gear themselves up by taking advantage of easier borrowing facilities. So the pace progressively quickens: more borrowing, more lending, more spending; second mortgages for home improvements; loans to companies for new and more productive plant and equipment. Everybody borrows to improve and 'capitalise their opportunities' (a distasteful phrase that last!).

New credit is spread like chaff in the autumn breeze. But when the props of easy money are pulled away, as in the backlash from the 1972/3 bonanza, the whole process works destructively in the opposite direction. Attempts to de-gear by liquidating purchases made on extended credit, and often at grossly inflated prices, inevitably coincide with reluctant – or departed – buyers and clamorous creditors. This is just one aspect of the money trap.

Such were the consequences of the property-cum-secondary-banking crisis of late 1973; the impasse of the financial fictionists who indulged in the fatal gamble of borrowing short-term and lending long. The parody of the short fuse up the trouser leg.

Exposure of the 'Good Times'

It is necessary here to interpose some provisos to what I stressed, right at the outset, as strictly academic explanations of some of the factors influencing investment method.

Because of avarice and ambition, both lenders and borrowers generate, in supposedly 'good times', an excess of cheap money. This is the response to reduced interest rates and the gaudy inducements, via the whole advertising media, to have it 'even better' than Macmillan's original exhortation. Credit is unendingly available (if at extortionate rates of interest) by way of banks' and stores' plastic plaques, plus the former's largesse, virtually down to the infant in arms. This is assumed astute commercial 'competition'. It was doubtless competitive to lend unstintingly to the Third World countries!

Excessive internal purchasing power, plus the cheap importation of totally frivolous consumables enabled by the same easy credit, can push any country's adverse trade balance to horrific heights. As I write now, in December '88, trade returns for November are just out – a deficit of £2.01 billion on the straight visible account, following the record £2.53 billion for October. Of this danger of overheating the Governor of the Bank of England has repeatedly warned, and so, if half-heartedly, have many others. But the media are *sotto voce* about such matters, solicitous for their almighty advertising accounts.

The Lamb and Its Tail

The three coupled influences – inflation, the interest rate, the external exchange rate in terms of competing currencies – these chase each other unendingly like the lamb its tail. This spring (1988) the UK interest rate has been cut successively, three times by ½%, down to a base 7½%. The reason, contradictorily, to deter the speculative stampede into sterling vis-à-vis notably the DM and the US dollar. Chancellor Lawson's burgeoning Budget, and the spur coming through to our exports imparted by a previously weak pound, have burned for our currency like a beckoning beacon in the international desert. Ironically, against the accepted edicts, for example the mounting trade deficit and the foreigners' illusion of a 'cheap' pound. A fortnight earlier it was evident that the despised US dollar was where the value really lay. And before we could draw breath the pound was prostrated and the dollar enthroned. Our base rate was promptly raised to 8% and since successively further to 13%. The lamb and its uncatchable tail . . .

Turbulent Force of Currency Speculation

One of the turbulent forces in the financial world, since the UK squarely entered the international arena, with its prime focus the God-given Greenwich meridian ('best of all worlds', as Norman Tebbit conceived) are the frenzied flights of hot money. Vast sums in foreign exchanges are switched around the world by the international currency speculators, virtually at the drop of a hat. Such has no allegiance to any quarter, and merely conforms to the best temporary refuge with the sole aim of instant profit; the motive for dealing at all has nothing to do with rational decision-making.

Huge currency switches between key financial centres can be in the above direct form, or, if intended on a longer-term basis, cloaked via bonds or internationally traded securities, without any attributes to serious investment. Take, for example, a leading international stock such as ICI. Such is transferable between the home market and other centres in the form of 'Depositary Receipts', now mainly American Depositary Receipts – ADRs. There are still now occasionally IDRs (International Depositary Receipts), but other forms have fallen out of usage. Put as simply as one can, they are given by banks expressing the deposit of securities. Such receipts are issued against the securities so deposited between one country and another, and are duly marketable in themselves.

*Vast sums in foreign exchange are switched
around the world*

I read at that time that the soothsayers of Shearson Lehman Hutton were suggesting a 12% base rate by the time of the completion of this effusion in late September – that is, of '88. This was commendably on target. The latest hoist, as I write, is to 13%, with the possibility of higher yet to come. This takes us back over the November 1978 level of 12½%, a level which had fallen in the same year to as low as 5%.

I thought these aspects of the exchange and base rate gyrations should be touched upon, because the movements are disruptive and distortive to normal investment practice.

Yardstick of Yield

Consider, in due turn, the fluctuating cost of money, and its influence on investment decisions, directly in relation to the market's stock-in-trade. Looked at from this aspect, equate the interest rate with yield – that is, what a stock or share returns annually by way of gross income: 'yield', 'return', 'income product', all one and the same. The multiplicity of quoted securities, ranging in finely graduated degrees of risk and reward, from British Government stocks downward to highly volatile deferred shares, are measured ideally, but by no means exclusively, by the yardstick of yield, with the emphasis continually shifting from one category to another in accordance with conditions.

Before the ravages of inflation falsified the yield structure of the market, there were fairly consistent differentials in income return as between the safest securities capitalwise, and the least safe, not to mention highly speculative. You rightly expected 12% for the lure of tropical abundance, where your rubber plantation might be engulfed by a typhoon overnight, but were comfortably content with 6% from an industrial 'blue chip' (first-class ordinary share). This overall gearing was traditionally enshrined in the yield ratio existing between, in the gilt-edged market, Old Consols, so beloved of the Forsytes, and the average for leading industrial ordinary shares, which usually offered at least twice as much in acknowledgement of their commercial risk.

Security, Risk, and Reward

Consider now the basic truth that it is the interplay of security, risk and reward, as influenced by the prevailing but constantly changing factors of politics, economics and finance, that should determine policy subject to (and I stress again) the individual's needs. For example, before the last war, if you had asked the average consultant to enumerate the basic principles of investment, you would doubtless have been told that one invested (a) for Security, (b) for Income, and (c) for Profit – in that unvarying order of importance. Further, you would have been instructed that both a high return of income *and* scope for profit were inconsistent with first-class security, although in numerous instances the former would logically go together. The more one sought after capital gain, it would have been stressed, the more automatically one sacrificed security.

But that was in the days of stable sterling, when the pound in your pocket regularly bought 20s worth of goods and services, and traders were duly obeisant to their customers. It was a buyer's market. Then the investor was income-conscious, solicitous for his capital because its income product had a more or less constant purchasing power. The aim was to preserve such capital by opting for security. Concern for physical possessions, notably house property, was that their value should be annually maintained rather than fortuitously increased.

Post-war inflation cynically inverted these commendable aims. Investors sacrificed security by going for compensatory capital gain. The theme of the latter 60s was the 'inflationary hedge' – pursuit of the dangled carrot of future reward generally in the form of free scrip (share) bonuses, to the exclusion of immediate yield. 'Growth' was thought to come up with the regularity of milk on the doorstep. It was in many phases of the market a case of the reluctant investor; in so far as the majority of people paid their shares the doubtful compliment of hanging on, it was because they saw themselves confined in a gilded cage by inflation-cum-Capital Gains Tax, and tried for a time cocking a snook at the taxman. Shares were for long preserved on an artificially high price plateau. The anti-inflation panaceas of successive governments accentuated this false position by exposing shareholders to all the risks, while largely denying rewards put in pawn to the future. Dividend limitation was a case in particular point.

Pre-war Options Well Defined

It will be seen, therefore, that, pre-war, the options open to the investor were reasonably well defined. Regularly recurring market cycles, up and down, on a two to three-year basis, constituted the pattern with a stable foreign trade and cheap imported food and raw materials; interest rates, via the old Bank Rate, automatically adjusted to nurse the economy along, and the Stock Exchange conformed at, on the whole, pedestrian pace. Because the currency was in no need of artificial propping with the baited hook of extravagant inducements to the overseas buyer, fixed-interest securities, notably the British Government Funds, enjoyed the status of impregnable security and maintained their correct yield ratio in relation to industrial ordinary shares, in which latter field investors largely confined themselves to the 'blue chips', except under boom conditions when they wandered precariously in the outfields of the market.

Subverting the Old Yardsticks

These then are the circumstances which, by insidiously subverting the old yardsticks of interest and yield, as among the qualifying factors in determining investment value, produced the oft-quoted 'reverse yield gap' – that is to say, debased Government stocks, like Old Consols and War Loan, lacking the backstop of a redemption date, until they were offering, at times, almost double as much as obtainable on the narrow range of industrial leaders. The distinction between bad money and good shares.

Having extolled all the fine old principles of investment, it seems a pity now largely to demolish them. At the same time, my purpose in contrasting conditions is to underline how, and why, the industrial equity became the focus of the post-war investment scene – but as a symptom, not as a cause, of events. As with so much else, the catalyst all along has been inflation. Whereas the Government stock, as a borrowing from the public in steadily eroding money, was clearly viewed as a wasting asset, with little attraction except as a medium for trading in at particular phases of the market, the hardcore of fixed assets represented by the big industrial companies, particularly those with overseas subsidiaries and earnings, plus land and property, were generally accepted as giving at least partial protection against inflation.

Speculators All

Whether we care to admit it or not, circumstances now compel the investor to become, in part at least, a speculator. Investment takes up a lot of time and study; prudent speculation, which is venturing one's own money, as distinct from gambling, which is venturing other people's money, takes infinitely more. Investment presupposes reasonable stability, not least in the currency; sufficient stability also in the trading position, in orders, wages, and material costs, to permit of a critical judgement on a company's fundamentals, at least in the medium term. But a calculated judgement such as this is largely impossible under conditions of inflation, however much we may care to dignify our purchases 'investments'. As just one aspect, we can see this in the effect of a soaring pound on overseas operators. Consequently, it is nowadays the height of folly to sit back, as one could in former times, on some eminent 'blue chip' sustained by the comforting conviction that, even were it to fall heavily, it would assuredly recover in the next upward cycle. Another consideration of the 'trap' is that, for all the high appraisal, the shares of such companies might not.

5

SEEDS OF CHANGE

What first stirrings, what undertow in the tide of new technology, led the Stock Exchange on the path of radical change? On this there will be diverse views.

In distant retrospect, I sense clearly where the seeds of change fell, although they may not have taken serious root at the time of dispersal. For example, the Visitors' Gallery, which project, it may surprise you, first commended itself to the Royal Commission on the Stock Exchange in 1877, was not, in fact, finally built until 1953. It was an instant success. With 1,119 visitors on the opening day, one newspaper of brash instancy, but no research, queried why such an 'admirable idea' had not been thought of years before!

Rapidly following the first step of its opening, a give-away leaflet was quickly prepared. I had put the question to my friend Gerald Hicks, of long-forgotten building materials jobber Charles Harris: why not, in view of the numbers passing through our portals, distribute a simple guide to what the viewer actually saw from his elevated position, the significance of what was happening below, an explanation of the market and its wares, its historical background? All easily digestible, in potted form, a sketch.

'Yes, why not?' pondered Hicks, who was on the Public Relations Committee. 'Let me have some jotted ideas for tomorrow morning. I'll put it up.' On a split open envelope discarded from the morning's post, I did a mock-up that evening of a two-way-fold leaflet with a bled-off crowd scene pasted on the front and a boxed title, in compliment to the visitor – YOU and the Stock Exchange. They accepted everything, except the frontage caption, mysteriously (I thought) inverting it to The Stock Exchange and You.

So that was how I came to devise the first publicity effort distributed from the Gallery, although there were to be many superior books and pamphlets to supplant it as the educative drive developed in the later 50s. Anyway, it is a droll instance of the delightfully relaxed attitude of the old convivial 'club' before professionalism laid its hand of pomposity. There are so many more tales which are today thought too incredible for belief. Such as (oft told by myself) how in 1968 I was summoned before Mr Wareham, then secretary of the Quotations Committee, to answer a priggish young member's complaint that Donald Cobbett was wantonly 'advertising' (then the eighth deadly sin among the Stock Exchange's Commandments) by putting my name to an article on House humour contributed to the leader page of the old *Evening News*. 'Look,' said Wareham, casually, 'help me to concoct a reply to this one.'

I have for years emphasised these bizarre tales of mine which are, I sense, complete anathema to those who now walk with great anxiety before the Financial Services Act.

With the trading floor quickly vacated post-Bang, the long-awaited Gallery, too, is closed down for its original purpose. As members and their dealers betook themselves to their tower-block offices to stare interminably at television monitors, there was, indeed, nothing left for a visitor to view except the Traded Optioneers attired like minstrels on the sands, and an entanglement of electric cabling and robot-looking gadgetry almost dwarfing the empty hexagonal stands. Ironical, as all this additional communications and computer

*Nothing left for the visitor to view except . . . an
entanglement of electric cabling*

dealing hardware was assembled only the year before, at immense cost to the market-makers. Not a few of these banker-broker conglomerates retired hurt from the initial free-for-all.

The interior area of the old Gallery, with its mini-cinema, was adapted and refurbished over a month, in June 1987, as a public information/instruction centre, with several of its ever-charming guides meantime indoctrinated in the technique of the new market, thereby to cosset and illuminate the visitor. Video screens and unfolding information tapes have since intrigued the would-be investor and riveted the already committed. As an aside, it was in the same year – 1958 – as our first information film, *My Word is My Bond*, was shown that the first three guides were engaged for the Gallery.

I would (were I permitted) be curious to learn what history records, when written on sober reflecting, of the abandonment of the London Stock Exchange's historic role, and the indecent haste with which the whole system and structure, built up over 300 years (should you look first to the founding of the National Debt), was extinguished with the immediacy of a snuffed-out candle.

As a result of its members' inauspicious retreat, London is now the only major financial centre in the world lacking a physical trading floor. A fact from which it seems incredible that the new, sparkling, hi-tech area officially opened by Her Majesty the Queen, with such a magnificent reception, on 8 November 1972, should within sixteen years have been rendered obsolete by the rapid march of computerisation.

We spoke jocularly then, at this opening of the imperiously risen building out of the descended rubble of the old. There was a viewing platform on Throgmorton Street from which the top-hatted could stare into the disembowelment of their beloved retreat. We quipped that the newly arisen trading floor, scene of that spectacular party, was destined for a species of supermarket or shopping precinct. But few of us suspected – so soon. Only Mr Harold Wilson, who astutely predicted that by the mid-80s it would be as relevant to our economy as a Cistercian monastery. He was spot on. Smith New Court, precursor of the famous jobbers Smith Brothers, gamely attempted a last-ditch stand, but themselves capitulated to the surrounding isolation in December 1986.

As with its long-delayed Gallery, the rebuilding of the Stock Exchange itself had long been mooted, mulled over, talked about and shelved, talked of more and shelved again, and largely regarded askance for reason of its steadily mounting cost. Even as the demolishers' picks began to swing in mid-1966, a Labour member of Parliament was asking the Minister of Public Building and Works to stop the work in view of the economic situation and the Government's curb on unnecessary building. Had it been another half decade on, he would have had a much more arguable case.

The first serious move towards rebuilding was ventured towards the end of the last war, when the official Surveyor, a Mr Buckingham FRIBA, relieved the tedium of his fire-watching by making plans for a complete reconstruction. The fruits of his labour were seriously considered, his original plan revised to meet the then Town Planning requirements, and in 1949 the City Corporation actually gave permission for development. Then the whole project, long deliberated on by the Building Sub-committee, was unanimously rejected by that same assembly, who recommended that rebuilding 'be not undertaken at present'. And the Council confirmed that decision.

Argued then that the old building was, in any case, solid and adequate to the needs of a membership considerably larger than it then was, it is clear that much of the pressure for rebuilding was a matter of keeping up with the Joneses in rearing glass and concrete. Everywhere around, the leading City institutions were thrusting to eternity in a forest of steel girders, and it was felt imperative by the bigger brass to enthrone us in equally grandiose style. By the time Sir Martin Wilkinson, by then chairman of the Stock Exchange Council, performed the 'topping-out' ceremony to mark the completion of the twenty-six-storey tower block on 15 July 1969, the authorities had long assessed the way things were going. Indeed, Sir Martin told me in 1971, in kindly commenting on an article I had prepared for *The Banker*, that we were steadily moving to the Continental situation, where most of the share dealing had been encompassed by the banks, albeit the bourses and share-markets preserved a façade.

By 1972 the edifice was up in all its £11 million-odd glory, but the coffers were sadly depleted. As the then deputy chairman remarked to me in 1974, following the first vicious hoist in Arab oil prices and the secondary banking/property débâcles, prostrating the whole market into a slump, 'There is currently a clamp-down on any additional expenditure . . .' One casualty to strict economy was the *Stock Exchange Journal*, first published in the spring of 1955.

If, ostensibly, the final curtain for the physical market was rung down in the concluding weeks of 1986, the real end for the elder generations, most of whom had lingered beyond their time in manning the House during the Second World War, was the weekend of 6/7 August 1966. This sounded the literal crack of doom. It was then that our main contractor, Trollope and Colls, commenced the first phase of the rebuilding.

Impossibly, a few of the diehards apparently sustained the illusion that, after all, it couldn't really happen. Inevitably it did. The House fraternity returned that Monday to find the die irrevocably cast. A 30-foot-high brick partition built from floor to ceiling divided off the easterly end of the 90-yard-long trading floor – that area notably beneath the historic Kaffir dome – from the gilt-edged and industrial markets. It was perhaps symptomatic of the Macmillan 'winds of change' that all the markets representative of African, Australian and Far

Eastern mining and tropical produce, plus the property pitches, were submerged beneath the descending rubble.

It was a further coincidence that as the older members began disconsolately to vacate their familiar scene, the vacuum was filled by the first arrival of post-war youth, those born in the late 40s. They came in, tousle-headed and colour-shirted, to the first stirrings of the Australian nickel boom. The heady Poseidon, initially obtainable for about 3s 6d, destined for £19 in the hothouse of Down Under gambling. On Christmas Eve 1969, a sudden meteor from the Outback, North Flinders, virtually doubled in price overnight from 25s to 50s. The voice of experience, had it been heeded at all, was steadily denied or derided. The indoctrination for the newcomers was to boom conditions.

So dawned the era of the 'boom babies', a genus from which today's yuppie has doubtless emerged. They were to bode no good for any of us. All manner of strange specimens then surfaced in the market-place, including one since much-publicised, of the Guinness entanglement. He was admitted an associated member in 1968, just about confirming my timing of the post-war entrants who were lured to a Throgmorton Street reputedly paved with gold, mesmerised by the mirage of easy money-making. With a smattering of experience, tender youth appeared with the millionaire's bankroll peeping, as he fondly imagined, from the corner of his shiny briefcase.

This was the age of the 'financial gun-slinger'. Indeed, at about this time an advertisement actually appeared in none other than the *Financial Times*, seeking just such an uninhibited marketeer for a fund management team. As I once overheard a youthful cynic observe, 'It's a licence to kill you need in Darkest Throgmorton Street today.' 'Anything that moves, buy it!' was the axiom of the boom babies, whose only view of the market was the upward curve on the charts and who brashly assumed, from the inflationary world in which they had been nurtured, that nothing ever went down significantly. And it was the same again in the case of the high-flying in the summer of 1987. Pricewise, it doesn't matter whether prices are pushing eternity. They'll buy it. In conditions of acute share shortage, and with big clients who don't mind gambling with the taxman's Gains Tax, it is possible virtually to write one's own price tags – so long as the game is kept in play.

In my early days, back in the 30s, it was a mature man's world to which the occasional youthful aspirant strayed – a world in which, of necessity, he was required to be seen and not heard. It was only the elderly, with something in hand from the boom times of the mid-20s, who could afford to endure the barren years around the turn of the 30s.

It was the elderly again, six years later, who were left to man the markets during the Second World War, which not only restricted new entrants, but drained away such of the younger generation as had earlier existed. Thus, historically, a generation that had, perforce, lingered beyond its time was largely swept aside by the flood of go-go youth, drawn to the market by the magnet of munificent salaries and bulging commission accounts. A revolution, some said. And those of us who could scarcely recognise a face at the bars agreed.

But perhaps the greatest paradox of those few years of booming stock markets was that, having made big money, the problem for the bosses of brokerdom had been how to find time off in which to enjoy it. For the administrators were involved in a paper chase which, as it then seemed, was destined to outpace them. In early 1971, for example, there was profound anxiety about the backlog of paperwork resulting from speculation in Australian mining shares. As a result, the Stock Exchange Council was forced to call for returns of unclosed Australian share deals. If that was the case then, how much more insuperable the administrative task today under the added burdens of surveillance.

To dismount from the interminable treadmill, on which the taxman relentlessly pursued the commission and profits, and had then himself to be chased anew in order to fulfil his demands, the urgent quest was for personal assistants. The appointments columns of the financial press were filled with appeals. 'Young, young, young', was the insistent plea of the personnel selectors, plus a vague concession to 'some experience' in their search for minions on to whose shoulders they hoped to unload the business burdens of their clients.

In this golden street, illuminated by all the good luck stories, it may be salutary to recall that it was not always the area of boundless opportunity as seen then, and perhaps yet again today, by the newcomers; those who fancy themselves permanently on to a good thing. As often as the booms, there have been the slumps – the bitterly barren years between, when the stock market was a turgid backwater in which shares stagnated, staff were sacked, and members resorted to practical joking to buoy their flagging spirits.

Nor was it held, in earlier times, in particularly high esteem. Galsworthy epitomises the Victorian attitude in *The Forsyte Saga* with his character Montague Dartie, the stockbroker, portrayed as an unrepentant bounder.

I can well remember my father telling me how, in the middle-class Victorian drawing-room, the Stock Exchange was regarded disdainfully as the 'home for lost dogs' – the last resort of the renegade son. At the family counsel on what should be done with Young George, rubicund Uncle Harry would finally burst in with the suggestion, 'Dammit, why not put the boy on 'Change!' So on 'Change, with his allowance cut off, young George reluctantly went, and eventually became Old George, who handled the family's business.

The father contemplating a career for his son – or, as it may equally be today, his daughter – will understandably envy the opportunities in bounding Throgmorton Street. His offspring will hardly be able to restrain themselves in the leap towards the executive chair, there to wield their ballpoints over the portfolios of a long-cherished clientele.

But it is a brash, brittle world, this world of stocks and shares. It is a world in which blind beggars on horseback abound, and private capital is at risk – and duly calls the tune. Imperious private ambitions, too, as we daily discover ... these more generally destructive than others. So, when the music stops, just watch out, because the bad luck stories are those most adroitly swept under the City carpet!

The other fundamental change in the structure of the stock market since the Second World War, more gradual, subtle, and infinitely more far-reaching in its effect, has been the encroachment on, and in the end total dominance of, the private investor by the institutional investor – this in the field of the industrial equity.

The sequence of events by which this trend evolved – the rising cost of living, the wages spiral, the virtual eclipse of the *rentier* through high taxation, and the steady channelling of small savings, premiums, contributions, and so on, to variously the building societies, unit trusts, life assurance offices, pension funds and trade unions, to name but a few non-personal investors, for handling on behalf of the public, as it were, by proxy – all are readily traceable and understood.

To this extent, the slow replacement of the individual by the institutional investor has been, and remains, a movement at once involuntary and inescapable. Like the individuals, the institutions tended right away from the early 50s to seek the inflationary hedge of the industrial equity, while, in an era of persistently larger capital demands, the diminishing financial capabilities of the public also shifted the responsibility of finding new working resources to the former. The resultant prominence, marketwise, of the big companies and conglomerates accelerated their growth and strength, in that new finance (borrowings or permanent capital) was more readily accessible, and on more productive terms, than to their smaller competitors.

Inherent in the redistribution of wealth, this fundamental change in the source, and consequent direction, of investment demand has had, in turn, consequences which have only latterly become fully apparent. While elevating the market leaders, it led, conversely, to the partial eclipse of the wider range of small-priced issues. The industrial market became, in effect, established on two distinct price planes. This fact placed the smaller concerns, no matter how sound their record, at a disadvantage, proportionately, in raising fresh finance, in that the retarding of their market capitalisations deprived them of the same scope for making new offers at a tempting premium. At the same time, this restrictive influence has undoubtedly rendered many more vulnerable to predators.

The gulf in size and consequent status, between big and small, has been dug deeper by the International Stock Exchange's classification of ordinary shares, graded downwards from the highly dealable alpha stocks to the admittedly often illiquid deltas.

If I have inflicted you here with some potted history, I apologise. Its purpose has been to impart background to much of what I write. Its essence is the underlining of the need for experience, and the suggestion that, with research, high value can still be uncovered in the shares of the small concerns. These in time must be absorbed as the market's stock-in-trade steadily contracts.

As an aside, vis-à-vis my comments above on the immense stranglehold of the institutional investor, it is instructive to note that, as a result of researches by the Metal Box Company in 1955, the total percentage of holdings definable as 'institutional' was given as 35.92%, which because of masked nominee holdings does not mean that the general public's participation was 64%. But when it is admitted by the company that individual investors now own only 13.5%, one can judge the extent of the instrusion of the institutions into issued equity capital. And this rate of control, probably 70% on average, would be common in the case of the major companies.

6

THE ILLUSORY ALADDIN'S CAVE

With the truism that 'What goes up must come down' goes the incontestable 'One person's gain is another's loss' . . . that is, so far at least as the stock market is concerned.

As I stressed in my first chapter, every newcomer to the stock market is seduced by the apparent ease of profit-making . . . that is, if he embarks on a steadily rising trend; and that is where the newcomers inevitably emerge. On the strength of one, possibly two, successive, quick, fortuitous 'tickles', they become convinced of the possession of the Open Sesame to an Aladdin's cave in Throgmorton Street.

This is the first, fatal mistake.

The further fact is that every newcomer, whether outside investor or insider minion, is conditioned subconsciously by his/her beginnings . . . the market climate in which they first start. If, like me, they entered in times of slump, they will always look back apprehensively over their shoulder at the long ascent out of the depths, sceptical of the façade of inflated prices, the brash talk at the bars; if they arrived in the heady days of boom without apparent end, they will reach instinctively for the stars with little or no instinctive caution. This was markedly the case with the post-war generation appearing in the late 60s, and again with the profit-sated speculators in the mid-summer of 1987.

The illusory Aladdin's cave

For myself, in every boom, as in every resultant slump, I have the feeling that this is where I came in. Although necessarily the precise factors affecting each market cycle are different, it might well be asked – if everything finally is so cut-and-dried, why don't we all make our fortunes? There are many strands in the pattern of the answer to this question, strands which entangle and ensnare the investor. These I will try gradually to unravel.

Well, for one illustration, take the following. At the two-thirds stage of the 1970–72 industrial boom, when outwardly the market was still going great guns, I recall a newly acquired, youngish client ambitiously declaring that *his* (he was most emphatic) investment criterion was a one-third profit on every purchase. My incredulous 'Oh!' he shed like water off a duck's back. He apparently expected me to produce the goodies from my topper with the regularity of a conjuror multiplying rabbits. I tactfully suggested that since the upwave seemed to be running out of steam, he would need to modify his ideas.

Eventually, of course, I lost that client.

As a further instance, not long after that, another novice newcomer, inevitably seduced by the runaway performance, made the fatuous observation that he was only interested in 'making profits' – by which, on the strength of a couple of quick, fortuitous 'turns', he apparently meant on the basis of Account speculation – in-and-out, no bother. Obviously, aren't we all? Accepting that assurance, I would not need to be pounding my typewriter. Clearly I was destined to lose another client. And duly did.

I wonder how many times I have written it? Hundreds, I should imagine: that anybody can make money, as easily as shelling peas, in a consistently rising stock market. But this simple truth is lost, as in the case of these erstwhile clients of mine, in the self-congratulatory euphoria of those who, on the strength of a few quick successes, become fatally persuaded that it is all so easy.

Advancing logically from this point, it is fortunate indeed for the stock market that it regularly deals for, and is advised and administered by, successive new generations of investors and attendant oracles. It arises from the fact that clients and practitioners alike are never either totally informed or totally disillusioned. Hence the continual put-'n'-take, the ebb and flow.

But consider. Were we to deal for an unchanging clientele who became with experience totally informed and disillusioned, obviously everybody would act in much the same way, and then there would be no opportunity. Consequently no stock market.

Equally, if we dealt in something of readily identifiable value, as in tins of beans reached down from a shelf by the retailer, instead of in enterprise, commerce and industry at, as it were, once removed, much the same would be true, because with a more precisely measurable value the scope for fluctuation – and opportunity – would be almost entirely eliminated.

As it is, we deal in industry, enterprise, commerce and ideas at second hand; the share certificate we acquire slightly obscures the reality of what we invest in. It follows from this that there is always a big area where what is positively known from the past, and what is anticipated for the future, mingle with intriguing possibilities and divers consequences.

To summarise these considerations, stock markets everywhere reflect not so much what things literally are, as what people *think* they are . . . or, among the optimists, devoutly *hope* they are. Two very different matters.

For this reason, stock exchanges everywhere are a continually distorting mirror showing only parts of the truth of their main ingredients – economics, politics, finances – in their constantly revolving proportions. According to the prevailing mood, therefore, prospects will be absurdly magnified at times, yet at others established facts from the past often

[64]

dwarfed, obscured, sometimes, surprisingly, totally ignored. And here is just one of the deceptions of the Aladdin's cave. Which of the siren voices is the most alluring – the fundamentals based on the past or the technical arguments for the future?

I should interpose here an explanation of the widely quoted P/E (price-earnings) ratio, because this is the measurement of value that best mirrors the vagaries of the popular opinion, hopes and fears, discussed above. And remember, do, that this is not the mirror of the individual's assessment of value, but the *averaged* assessment of the participating public, necessarily including hundreds of shareholders who know intimately, perhaps positively, the fortunes, current and potential, of the company concerned. Which is not to suggest that even they are correct. The company's factory could be burned down overnight.

The P/E ratio is technically the ratio of the ruling ordinary share price to the last annual distributable earnings per share – that is, to make it abundantly clear, the net available earnings after corporation tax and prior charge distributions. Expressed perhaps more pictorially, the P/E expresses the number of years it would take to 'buy' the particular company in its entirety, on the basis of the last available net profits, at the ruling market capitalisation. In the not so distant past, eminently important companies have languished for months on buy-out levels of five or six times profit.

Regarded in isolation from accompanying yardsticks of value, the P/E can be highly deceptive; it can impart an inverted impression of value – or the reverse. Buyers who run away after the dangled carrot of future reward will drive the ratio high, say to 30, 40, 60 even 70, in total disregard of immediate income return, thus discounting prospects for years ahead. Equally deceptive is the unduly low or persistently languishing P/E, token alternatively of an uninspiring trading record or a positively suspect position and prospect. Such shares, especially the latter, will often be found to offer an exaggeratedly high income return, a mirage, of course, since the dividend is likely, at best, to be cut; at worst, passed. Very high or very low P/Es should be critically assessed for being a distortion of the truth due to our old factor of over-optimism or over-pessimism.

Before my deviation into P/E ratios, I was discussing the magnification or debasement of company facts. Many times I have known the published truth of a company's position lie squarely before the public for months, and yet go totally unrecognised. A blind spot in the analytical mind. As one very pointed example of this type of omission, I recall, back in early 1961, Klinger Manufacturing, a nylon stocking manufacturer then just beginning the development of a synthetic fibre processing machine destined to eclipse the original method of stocking manufacturing. The chairman, as I recall, flew the facts and advantages of this technical advance from the topmast in his annual statement. On this the shares could only move grudgingly from about 7s 6d to around 9s. In 1964, on a straight comparison, they touched a peak of 76s. It took, as it so often does, an unconscionably long time for the penny to drop. On both fundamentals and technical analysis, there are today many industrial shares languishing in or near the bargain basement. Yet they go unrecognised by those experts continually combing the market for new value.

For the private investor, I should now add that slavish attendance on your stockbroker is not the Open Sesame to success. Those who camp out on his office doorstep will, more than likely, confuse themselves in their proximity with the hub of affairs. Almost inevitably the once self-acclaimed investor will find himself converted into an opportunist trader, suffering more in expenses than achieving in profits, and unwittingly discarding his originally sound selections for precarious speculations. Particularly on a solid, primary rise, you may sacrifice far more than you secure by switching horses; what you exchange into is unlikely to be better than, if as good as, what you originally held.

Conversely, the reticent investor who works meditatively, well removed from the distractions of cluttered events, and, as earlier suggested, deals through a less harassed 'country' stockbroker, is likely to do better than the office-haunting City ferret down too many holes at once. The student in deepest Dorset will, above all, have time to read and inwardly digest. Intelligent reading of company reports, and especially chairmen's annual (or interim) statements, will often reveal germs of information from which the imaginative can draw conclusions. If for reasons of prudence they do not lay everything out, as in the case of my illustration with the erstwhile Klinger Manufacturing, chairmen largely tell the truth, and the diligent assembly of minor facts ignored by the financial interpreters can frequently put the private investor on the right track. He learns, for example, that Case and Parcels stores, while not enjoying the luxury of a freehold site on a suburban broadway, at least has the shared potential of a greyhound track bordering its transport garages and at a distance of 200 yards down the same side road. So he picks up the shares of the greyhound company to salt away for the future. Here, perhaps, could be the magic word!

Another potential money trap of which the newcomer must be aware is the short-cut style of modern business. The initiative now comes largely from the fund managers, who tend, because of their intensely competitive positions and the current passion for performance, to act in unison, and rapidly to change their minds. In short, the big difference from earlier times lies in the fact that whereas the then dominant private investors were usually both buyers *and* sellers, using individual judgement, the institutions now tend to be either buyers *or* sellers. This is the reason for the present-day tendency for instant boom and instant slump, and the necessarily abrupt one-way price swings and vast gyrations in the indices. In the past, the business, up and down, was cushioned by rival opinions; the index change at the session's close would generally be confined to a few points. Although admittedly today the business is in large volume, it is in far too few hands, and is turned on and off by the self-styled experts like a tap from a main.

With this pattern of business, it is only too easy for the small investor to be caught consistently moving off the wrong foot by way of a put-'n'-take performance. The only prudent course, if any is really advisable today, is to avoid being siphoned in on the rise or scared out on the mark-back.

7

YARDSTICKS OF VALUE

Enthusiastic newcomers to the stock market are often deluded by the assumption of some 'insider' formula giving entry to a succession of infallible selections. They fancy that by a mastery of assembled facts and figures, impressively presented arithmetically, they will be magically possessed of the incantation.

'Oh, you know what to buy, I dare say,' probes the investor, raising a quizzical eye. 'After all, *you're* in the market.' And he gives a penetrating look, as if he can see the rare goodies secreted about your person.

Looked on as brashly as this, little is further from the truth. Such simple alchemy as there may be in share-spotting is rather, in my view, the precept: 'safe, not sorry'.

'For heaven's sake,' mutters the present-day oracle, wet behind the ears in experience, but moist of palm with constrained conscience, 'let's keep to the straight and narrow, do . . .' Here, indeed, is where a studious analysis of the fundamentals – those mundane facts and figures dredged from the past – is essential in avoidance of the more obvious pitfalls. Yet as I have several times already stressed in these pages, market forces too often throw discretion to the prevailing wind. To this extent nothing is wholly insulated against, nor necessarily excluded from, the market's primary moves.

With the growing 'do-it-yourself' persuasion compelled to have an ever wider eye to the burden of expenses, we can expect a greater personal ready-reckoning and study of the yardsticks of value, in assessment of share potential.

Already in the previous chapter I have dealt with perhaps that most important measure of value – the P/E ratio – the rating on popular opinion. It is now necessary to amplify this lead (or maybe detraction) with some other critical considerations. So, what do we look to next? Say, first, w-well . . . ?

The truth is you could seek enlightenment of a dozen experts, but would not necessarily get a uniform opinion on first essentials.

Five-year Record

Yet most, I fancy, would look for viability as an operator . . . whether, profitwise, a progressive company, retrogressive, static, an irregular performer, or patently down the pan? For this guidance they would look first to the five-year record customarily condensed, for the convenience of the sharehol-der, right at the end of the accounts. Such figures may mean little in isolation, but a great deal in succession and thereby on comparison.

Vital Profit Margin

In consideration of the ordinary share, as we necessarily are here, the first concern is with growth. The first observance, therefore, is not only the long-term trend of the money turnover on the top line, but the relationship of these succes-sive figures to the resultant second-line pre-tax operating profits (losses) – and, incidentally, before interest and depreciation.

Obviously, in times of persistent inflation, you may have a rising money turnover (conceivably even from shrinking sales of products and/or services), and parallel static or eroding profits. The first simple indication of the vital profit margin. But look beyond any divergence between money turnover and pre-tax profit for the possible explanation – deteriorating or energised management; a new or more lucrative product or activity; inclusion of a new business; losses or write-offs on discontinued activities. Of particular significance is the position where the operating profit jumps (or falls) sharply out of line with the previous pattern generally. Look to directorial comments for some explanation. If none, look doubly in depth at the company's trading.

Standing of the Ordinary Shares

Beyond a consistent and, hopefully, rising profits trend, most look next to the standing of the relative ordinary shares themselves as a measure of public confidence.

There are several aspects here. First, the 'high'/'low' price range over the year concerned: are the shares standing near their peak, in the trough, or wherever, compared with the extremes ascertainable from the serious dailies? For a big price swing, again seek an explanation.

Second, what percentage income return (yield) is offered the current purchaser annually on the outlay? How does this compare with the average return from others in the same sector of the market? How does it compare with the net yield obtainable, risk-free as to capital outlay, from a building society? Is the industry represented as a whole progressive or languishing? And, perhaps most important, to what extent is the full year's dividend disbursement covered by available profits – that is, cover for the net distribution plus the attributable tax credit. Put another way, 'cover' is the ratio of the profit, after tax and prior charge obligations, to the ordinary dividend. Example: if the profit is £1.2 million and the ordinary dividend requirement £400,000, then the dividend cover is three times.

Of the entanglements the newcomer seems to get into in weighing the simple 'yardsticks of value' set out in the *Financial Times*'s price columns, the greatest perplexity, I find, arises from attempts to reconcile the dividend expressed in *net pence per share* with the parallel 'yield' representing the *gross percentage* return at the ruling market price of the shares.

Everybody, it must be remembered, does not suffer income tax at the same rate, if at all; some pay varyingly more than the standard rate. The quoted 'yield gross' allows for adding back to the net figure the standard tax deducted (now 25%). To this extent, those who do not conform to the average know better where they stand.

How do you most easily convert the actual pence payment into the gross percentage yield – termed 'grossing up'? First, by multiplying the net pence paid per share by 100 and dividing by 75. Then you must relate gross pence as a percentage of the nominal (par) value of the shares. For simplicity, take ICI, represented by £1 shares standing, as I write, at roughly £11. The past year's net dividend of 41.0p becomes, on our calculation above, 54.66p. As a percentage of 100 you have the same number, and applying the simple formula for current yield per cent (multiplying the nominal value by the gross percentage dividend, dividing by the ruling market price), you get:

$$\frac{100 \times 54.66}{1{,}100\text{p}} = 5\% \text{ gross yield}$$

*How do you most easily convert the actual pence
payment into the gross percentage yield?*

This the rounded-up figure in my current, *FT*, which does not pursue decimal points with its gross yields.

Nominal or Par Value

The other question I am most frequently asked concerns the nominal (equally termed par) value – and its frequent absence from the price columns of the *Financial Times*. 'Why,' ask the perplexed, 'are there often no basic share values shown?' But there are. It is the common practice nowadays to assume all UK ordinary shares to be of a 25p nominal value (as most are), unless otherwise specified, and the paper's explanatory notes stress this fact. The exceptions range widely from 1d to £20 shares, in which cases the nominal values are entered. (By the way, do read the 'notes', without which interpretation is difficult.)

There is, too, the apparently mystifying colloquialism known as 'closing' – that is, doing a reverse deal, buy or sell, to close up an earlier transaction within the *same* Stock Exchange Account and in the *same* number of shares. This is the only remaining concession cost-wise: 'nil to close' in the matter of commission – nothing further on the closing bargain.

The 'Account'

Your transaction, described rather ambiguously as a 'bargain', buy or sell, is always done for a specific Stock Exchange Account, and for the Settlement (Pay-day) relative to that Account. Dealings in gilt-edged stocks are generally for cash settlements, i.e. on the next working day. The normal fortnightly Settlements are phased ahead to the Monday-week following the end of each Account, and the date of the Settlement is clearly shown on the contract note. Statements of debtors are usually dispatched on the Wednesday before the Settlement; those in credit receive their statements of account with accompanying cheques on or around Pay-day.

It is necessary to insert here that the Stock Exchange 'Calendar' is divided into twenty-four Account periods, twenty of which are of a fortnight's duration, while four are three-week Accounts spread throughout the year to span public holidays.

What Do the Two Accounts Basically Mean?

Carried a stage further, if you, as a shareholder, are to get the best from the increasingly more comprehensive company reports available today, you will need to have some idea of the underlying principles and concepts that govern the preparation and presentation of the published balance sheets and profit and loss accounts, plus accompanying auditors' comments thereon.

The *Profit and Loss Account* is in essence a statement of the revenue earned during the period concerned, and the charges which should be matched against it to determine the net surplus to meet the payment of dividends and to carry forward a credit balance to provide additional funds for financing further development. A company which can sustain its momentum and growth out of earnings, as distinct from having to raise additional working capital, is in the most desirable position.

. . . And the *Balance-sheet*? It can best be visualised as a kind of financial snapshot which at the end of the financial year transfixes the circulation of money within the business, showing the sources from which its funds have been derived and the uses to which they have been applied. It is a statement of the ever-revolving capital position.

Shareholders' Funds

Touching on capital raises the description 'shareholders' funds'. Broadly, these comprise the issued and fully paid-up share capital, reserves in various categories, and retained profits; these together, representing the company's liability to its shareholders, must balance with what they are owed – the net tangible assets. Remember what I have just written about 'revolving capital' within the balance-sheet, because these figures embrace the working resources – the surplus, hope-fully, of current assets over current liabilities used to finance the day-to-day business.

   Look always for real liquidity in cash and readily cashable items among the current assets; and among the liabilities, any emergence of a bank borrowing or suspiciously large increase in a past borrowing. The only comment here is that a company sitting uninspiringly on a cash pile may be as questionable for its inactivity as one over-extended – and over-borrowed – in new developments.

Capital Gearing

Preoccupation with the dividend and the wherewithal for its provision must not be allowed to exclude the company's capital obligations, originally on the initial public offer or as subsequently enlarged. Increased profit visualised from a new investment could change the capital structure, so diluting or enhancing the benefit. Ideally, it could be financed from past retentions – real growth. Equally, it might necessitate fresh borrowing or perhaps a 'rights' issue from a proportion of up till then unissued capital.

Capital structure is certainly among the first considerations to weigh in the analytical scales . . . particularly the 'gearing' of the *borrowings* (debentures, loan stocks) in relation to *permanent* (preference and ordinary) capital. *High gearing* is in the form of borrowing in greater proportion to ordinary share capital: beneficial to the latter when trading is buoyant; sharply divergent in adverse times. *Low gearing* is precisely the reverse. The gearing ratio is calculated by a division of the fixed-interest capital into the issued ordinary capital.

Measuring a Company's Worth?

Now we know a few of the principal aspects of the balance-sheet, we should consider how this information can be interpreted when assessing a company's worth as an investment. But remember, accounts in the form in which they are presented can only mirror the past, whatever hints may be derived as to the future.

The individual will obviously base a preliminary assessment of the representative share on the rate of return which the dividend offers on the personal holding, conditioned by knowledge of alternative investment possibilities. However, the market price may vary from day to day, and is influenced by factors not strictly relative to the company's performance.

From the longer viewpoint, in assessing the degree of success with which a business employs its resources, a more significant basis for comparing performance is to judge it by the rate of profit earned on the capital employed. This is perhaps the primary financial ratio by which a firm can be judged effectively, and so long as the limitations of this method of appraisal are recognised, it offers a valuable yardstick which, by definition, is the best test of worthiness.

Business Ratios

As is generally stated, the book value of fixed assets (property, plant, machinery, etc.) may not be a reliable guide to their current value, and in cases where an undervaluation exists it may give a more favourable comparison with similar businesses than is justified by the true value of the assets employed. Additionally, the usefulness of the *return on capital employed ratio* as a method of inter-company comparison can be nullified by the various methods which firms use to finance their acquisition of fixed assets.

Accounts Inevitably Outdated

In the intervening period between a company's year-end and the publication of its full report and accounts, time has to be allowed for closure of the books following the declaration of the dividend; for the completion of the audit work; and for publication of the requisite notice to convene the Annual General Meeting, by which time the full accounts will have been approved by the directors for circulation to the members (equally meaning shareholders). In all, for a company concluding its trading year on, say, 31 December, allow that the AGM might not be held until early June. Then the final dividend would be confirmed by the meeting – and paid. Interim dividend payments require only the sanction of the directors in session.

8

THE WORLD WHERE NOTHING PLEASES

Any attempt to keep abreast of events (even such as publication lag permits) must inevitably fail by such a margin as to appear ludicrous to the eventual reader. But I stressed in the opening of my preface the speed of the water under the bridge. Yet there are points for instructive comment from the now over-two-year experience of Big Bang theory. Always when markets are subjected to a species of refinement by fire, the ultimate effects – educationally, at least – may well be as salutary as their immediate consequences were disconcerting.

First of all, in a 'bear' (downward) phase, such as we experienced in the spring and summer of 1988, it is a world where nothing, absolutely nothing, pleases. It seldom has in similar circumstances. You could stand in Throgmorton Street offering a pound for a penny, and everybody would look askance. You may scarcely believe me without reference far back, but as an illustration, Rothmans International 'B' ordinary shares were obtainable in early January 1975 at 14½p, less than the price today of the proverbial 'pound of tea'. But then there were hundreds of price absurdities.

On this last occasion, in October 1987, the jolt from the backfire was felt by as many seasoned operators as totally inexperienced dabblers, and I mean whether private or institutional. Indeed, after seven years of insistent boom there were perhaps relatively few of the so-called 'seasoned' acclimatised to such a chill wind of adversity. To the extent that it was instant fallout, the impact was the more profound. The illusory attitude of the 'experts' is a subject, in itself, for psychological study. How could they have failed to assess the absurdity of that summer's 'Balaclava Charge'?

The answer is, I respectfully suggest, because variously of the fatal 'short-termism' of the City's new breed of fund manager, under the whip of the 'performance' cult, the pitiful ignorance of the new 'popular' investor lured to the market by privatisation tinsel, and the loathsome greed of the manipulative interests generally, in keeping the bandwagon running full-tilt to the very brink of disaster.

In explanation of the enthusiasm with which we all emerged from the Second World War, I can well remember writing that so long as everyone was busily and profitably engaged, they did not see – and did not intend to see – beyond their noses. This was the case at that time, and has been the case on so many occasions since.

In view of what I have already written, I wonder who is plagiarising whom if I quote briefly from an article in the *Investors' Chronicle* by John Campbell, about a subject on which I have vigorously expounded. The article (1–7 July 1988) is on the short-sightedness of fund managers, and the paragraph I found most apropros of my own opinion, as under:

> In essence, the accusation against the City boils down to inveterate 'short-termism'. Industrialists complain that analysts and investors alike have little interest in major projects with a long-term pay-off, and are positively hostile if the cost involves short-term diminution of earnings and profits. Since punishment, in the shape of lower share prices, can lead to a hostile takeover, managers are often deterred from taking the right long-term decisions for their companies. When bids do come, the City is all too ready to accept a quick buck from wheeler-dealers and financial sharks rather than to back experienced management already in place. The ultimate loser is the British economy.

The final words above I find much in tune with what I wrote in the final searing chapter of my *Before the Big Bang*, in arguing that this Tory Government's concern to cultivate an international market here in London was to reinforce the façade of invisible exports by financially generated services, to the detriment of our hardcore heavy industry. I added . . . '*A travesty against the human wreckage left in the trail.*'

Black Monday is, of course, indelibly imprinted on the mind, destined to be recalled over the years with the enormity of the Hatry crash on 19 September 1929 . . . or the bursting of the South Sea Bubble in 1720. It is certainly imprinted on mine, having just arrived for a break in Sorrento out of the teeth of the Friday's tornado. I was lingering in the hotel's marbled hall when stragglers from a financial seminar of elated Italian businessmen chanced by. Learning that I was sometime of the London bourse, they sought my opinion of the prospects and apparently judged me in an advanced state of imbecility. I remarked that I would touch nothing even with the end of a gondolier's barge pole.

I had met with the same blank, unbelieving tolerance when I expressed some deprecating views on the market on 29 September. I had been invited to talk to a group of investors at the Institute of Directors, Pall Mall. Somewhat poker-faced and uncomprehending, this mainly male assembly sat stolidly through an avalanche of gloom. Whether or not they believed a word, I cannot say, but they had then about three weeks in which to make their escape. Or was their reconciled attitude due to the fact that they had already abandoned ship?

Looking back, I can see conveniently, in the mind's eye, the broad diagram of the market's trend; its repetitive ups and downs, from the cavernous depths to the very cannon's mouth. And of all the 'bull' markets I have experienced, none compares in length with the seven-year run (some may judge it thirteen) to the dizzy peak of 1926.2, by the measure of the *FT* ordinary index, touched on 16 July 1987. Absurdity of absurdities. It seems incredible that the analytical experts, in which the City allegedly abounds, could not foresee, clear as crystal, the consequences of gross over-indulgence. The fact that they did not is largely because, as earlier suggested, they did not want to.

Although there was no comparable measurement at the time, I fancy the closest rival in upswing cycles could well have been the 1920s industrial boom, fired off by the popular motor car, the gramophone, the humble 'cat's whisker', greyhound racing, and embracing the famous 'dirt-track' market in the 'penny dreadfuls' of the day. All of which boiled over with the customary unhappy consequences in the Hatry crash and the following Great Slump. Poor Clarence Hatry! Twelve solid years, wasn't it? I often think, what a pimple on the pompous escutcheon of the almighty City compared with the running sores of today's multiple miscreants!

But however long my personal recollections, confirmation by the ISE's *Quality of Markets* statisticians proves me correct in picking 1975–87 as incomparably the longest running boom experienced on the London market. They pointed out that this was a consensus of opinion, and asked whether I was viewing the overall rise in terms of the primary trend, ignoring intermediate fluctuations on the way up. This was my view, and on that basis the upswing spanned roughly twelve and a half years.

Returning to the length of the 1920s upwave, given the acceleration imparted by the 1924–5 rubber boom, high activity ran on, if my memory serves, for a good seven years. So it is a creditable runner-up. The awed 'Great Slump' was really of comparatively short duration. By the mid-summer of 1933, when, incidentally, I first entered the market, we were pulling out of the worst. Then, again, there was a steady upswing, if less spectacular (except in Rhodesian coppers and wayout gold shares . . . those of the West African 'Jungle' and Westralian sectors), until we came increasingly under the

The 1920s industrial boom, fired off by the popular motor car

shadow of threatening war. By about 1937 little further progress could be made with Hitler's continual sabre-rattling. There was no panic; the market just drifted insidiously lower. (You can trace the point of reversal clearly in the diagram below.) At best an uninteresting phase, which left the index around 80 by the time I was called to the RARO in August 1939.

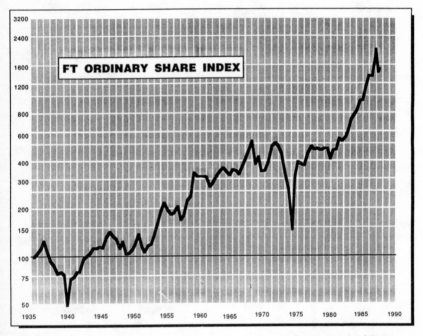

Source: *Financial Times*

The diagram is reproduced by kind permission of the *Financial Times*, whose editor I cajoled into assenting to my request, a long-range graph of their 30-share ordinary index, from 1935 until mid-1988. In view of the kindness just acknowledged, it may seem churlish to remark that, having specifically asked for long-range, the graph-line is necessarily strong as a visual impression, and thus indecisive as to precise detail. For example, the September 1968 peak was 521.9, and the May 1972 peak 543.6. The graph suggests the former as the higher.

Allowing for the above, if you study carefully you can pinpoint the passage of events from the primary trendline ... most pointedly the Second World War collapse of June 1940 (Dunkirk and the index's all-time 'low' of 49.4); next the calamitous freefall from the May 1972 peak of 543.6, all the way down to the depths of 146.0 in early January 1975 ... a two-and-a-half-year downward cycle. But how precipitous! I then wrote in my feature in Eire's financial weekly journal, *Business and Finance*:

> There can be only two views now of our stock market here – either it is predicting a catastrophe too horrendous to contemplate or industrial shares are cheap beyond comparison ...

But no credit to me, because I had by then just glimpsed the opinion of that Welsh financial wizard, Julian Hodge, who publicly stated that he personally was acting on that principle. The market began gradually to stabilise virtually from that point.

The major cycles, up and down, are stark enough. But what are instructive for the beginner, anxious to learn from experience, are the minor reflections. For example, the breath of relief on the fragile majority of 5 overall secured by the second post-war Labour Government in the 1964 general election; the indecisive pause after their more positive re-election in 1966 (majority then 97), enabling enactment of the dreaded Capital Gains Tax. You can trace the hiccup of anxiety in the trend.

At just around this point in time there is an excellent example of the public's sensitivity to the spark of inspiration when the market seems in a no-go at any price mood. I well recall then the occasion of Unilever's three-quarter-year preliminary figures which appeared, as customary, in early

November 1966. Up until then there had been disenchant-ment with Labour's re-election, and an insipid slide in the market. By the autumn of 1966, the *FT* ordinary index marked its 'low' of 289.

Then the transformation, the tinkling cymbal as already related. Like building materials, food manufacturers and retailers provide a pivotal pointer to the way of the wind. Food is a bedrock purchase, and ''arf o' marge' in the shopping basket about the most basic call there is on the family purse. Big in fats, the dominant Unilever then came out with better than expected profits. This put new heart into the market at just the psychological moment to evoke a popular response.

Look now at our graph around end-1966: from there, barring hiccups, there is an uninterrupted runaway up to the crucial double-top formation described over November–December 1968. Those two years were the locked-in years of constraint in the gilded cage of Socialist dogma, not least in the form of the Capital Gains Tax which took effect from 6 April 1965. If holders did not pay their shares the compliment of actually liking them, they generally of necessity sat tight. There was worse outside the shield of corporate assets burgeoning to eternity, so they felt, in the hot-house of rabid inflation. There was also the hot breath of the taxman, at whom it was elected to cock a perpetual snook. So people obstinately held on, available share supplies were inherently short, and the edifice of accumulating reward so grew steadily higher.

To pass on a few years, where I can perhaps lay claim to some judgement, both ways, was with the relatively truncated 'bull' cycle following the June 1970 re-election of a Conser-vative Government. This upswing lasted a little over twenty months from its first stirrings in mid-1970 until mid-May 1972. If short, it was sharp, particularly in its final outburst. After hammering home over several months my anxiety about the 'dangerous deception of boomtime stock markets . . .', I opened my commentary in the 18 May 1972 issue of *Business and Finance* (I was still writing my feature), with the following tirade:

> Readers may have noted my increasing concern for the market in recent months. It was, I have felt for some time, over-extended and brashly-bought; it was holding itself up on the strength of its past momentum, an effort difficult to sustain without helpful factors, let alone a succession of crises. It was thin and tired, a combination which always behoves caution.

On the very next day, Friday 19 May, the industrial market touched its then all-time peak and from there on fell steadily away, with massive acceleration in the final stages, to the 1975 'low'. As the reader will note, a token of the near bottom in any collapse is the rate of the fall (largely an evasive/panic mark-down) in the final phases. Such will be followed, as earlier explained, by the 'plateauing' period of indecision reached in the abyss.

In the above-mentioned upward cycle, as in all others, the circumstances were the precise opposite to those discussed at the start of this chapter. Then the scenario was of a *world where everything pleases*, the prospect viewed through ever rosier-tinted glasses, with the bad news swept assiduously under the carpet. It is truly amazing how much bad news can be surmounted in a really heady market. Hurdles of seeming disaster (then a crisis of strikes, including the miners', the nearing US débâcle in Vietnam, a rampant 'bull' market in which too few brains were chasing too much money) are taken with agility.

Now, another lesson in long-term anticipation. If the majority were distinctly disenchanted with most things on the down-trail from the '69 peak, a few were sufficiently astute to sense that the one really moribund market – that in shipping shares – could come to the fore as a compensator. So in time it did. One of the few really brilliant opportunities of that troubled decade; more spectacular, in a sense, but with infinitely less risk, than the dominating Down Under nickels. For one example, Graig Shipping's £1 ordinary shares steamed ahead from a little over 20s to around £24. As good as, perhaps better than, the legendary Poseidon?

It was still the case, in those days before the complete dominance of these fund managers, that markets were in individual hands. There were separate shipping jobbers, rubber jobbers, jobbers in copper and other mining issues, etc., so many independent 'books', without involvement elsewhere with wider interests or capital committed around other markets. And to this extent, an independent and introspective sector could respond to its particular events and often move in flat contradiction to the common trend. How perverse, they might say today!

It has not, I hope, evaded your notice that I am still demonstrating the practical lessons of timing and anticipation. Please keep referring to the graph to parallel what I am trying to convey.

In remarking on my scepticism about the overheated run-up to the May '72 peak, I mentioned getting it right both ways. This was infinite luck. In fact, I had been tenaciously pointing the recovery from mid-summer 1970, encouraged by the fact that the mighty Prudential had, I was told, been quietly picking up stock that August.

Of tramp (dry cargo) shipping shares, a remarkably hard sell because of an obsession with the long post-Suez slump in freight rates to the exclusion of their subsequent partial recovery, I had been an ardent enthusiast since 1965. I reckoned that this sector had gone largely unrecognised, except for the liner issues, and that share prices were bumping along the bottom and extremely refined technically. There were few weak 'bulls', little available stock at the then levels, and such tired holders as there were were involved so much higher up in the price scale they were unlikely to impede any advance in its initial stages. These are always the sort of considerations to weigh when assessing recovery potential.

With my New Year greetings for 1970, I see on referring back that I was well away on my tramp theme with a caption – 'Sailing into the Seventies' – having already pointed out in end-October that 'Tramp shipping freight rates have already now risen to new peaks for the year in most trades; an explosion has occurred in the price of second-hand tonnage . . .' In mid-November I was underlining this with: 'The ascendancy of the shipping sector over the remainder of the market has special significance in these times of liquidity disasters at almost every turn . . . The simple reason for this opposing strength is that the shipping industry, as a carrying service, is not so bedevilled by rising costs . . .' And so on, intermittently, for many months.

I was not alone, but certainly in the forefront of those share selectionists in unflagging pursuit of this section well into 1971, by which time considerable profits could have been secured.

Now, moving abruptly to the present, I am amazed, on hardly any reflection at all, at the short-sightedness/ gullibility/ineptitude – whichever you choose – of those who, with recent events stuck squarely beneath their noses, could so inexplicably misjudge and miscalculate.

After the beckoning Budget of March last, the CBI crows its overall contentment, the Chancellor eulogises on his financial and economic successes (many of which admitted), the DoT preens its plumage . . . and the stock market treats the lot with scepticism, if not derision.

Daily, too, one reads with wonder of the munificent profits achieved by companies, big and small, yet their representative shares, if tempted to flutter feebly, quickly retreat amid the first plaudits. Is it perhaps the teenage scribblers 'pencilling in' new 'numbers', and picking holes in the past imperfect?

Wasn't the US dollar at somewhere about $1.8960 to the pound sterling, only in end-May, incontestably the best buy in the world? But nobody apparently was prepared to say so, except talk impossibly about $2, and flutter about abstractedly in their views like suicidal moths around a candle flame. And this one of the most recent omissions of almost inevitable profit. But, as I observed at the start of this chapter, *absolutely nothing* pleases.

9

CLIMATE OF THE UNSTOPPABLE

. . . And what of the small investor now?

(I intended titling this chapter 'Martyrdom of the Minions', but discarded it as too dramatic even for my typewriter.) But the 'small investor' . . . yes, that is my unending theme, and, I think, rightly, the theme of most financial commentators.

The extract from the last chapter in my previous paperback quoted in the second chapter here, predicting the likelihood of a greatly diminished, perhaps eventually even a wholly one-way, market in many capital issues, was among the vital problems I foresaw for those emerging from the past with part of their wherewithal inextricably frozen in by lack of market-ability in the modern form. That this has turned out to be so can scarcely be denied.

I dare say that like paint of a similar but different shade, my dislike of the whole concept of Big Bang grins through, as the decorator would describe. I never relished the prospect of 27 October 1986, and I have disliked the subsequent practice infinitely more. While taking care to distance myself as far as possible from what was my whole life, I cannot believe that the future will ameliorate my attitude to, nor my enduring per-ception of, this new-style Vanity Fair.

In letters to a kind respondent in the Companies Legisla-tion Division of the Department of Industry, back in the earlier 80s, I ventured to suggest that post-Bang would see more financial fraud than we had ever suffered in the past. To which impertinence, I was granted the observation (I quote) that were my ... 'vision of post-reform securities dealing to become reality the outlook would be pretty gloomy'. I find it difficult now to reconcile the verb 'reform' with the recent conduct and excesses in the Square Mile – and beyond. However, 'gloomy' indeed it has become, as I fancied. With an endless series of entanglements and intrigues – open arrests, sentences, extraditions, sackings, dismissals, suspensions, background involvements – down from so-called 'blue-blooded' broking houses, merchant banks and accountants, to the lowest little shysters in the business environment, who can seriously disagree? The front-page columns of the responsible Press are daily crammed with their calumnies and deceptions, cast in ever deepening dye.

Could anyone, for example, have remotely imagined that, with cautions rife from a quarter of the highest eminence in accounting circles, the Barlow Clowes Gilts circus could have been suffered for two months, let alone two years, after 'serious warnings' of irregularities, if one may accept the Press revelations?

Back in late 1983, before completion of the Gower Report on investor protection, the DTI was asserting that it was unlikely that ... *'this department would sanction any development in the market likely to increase the possibility of dishonesty'*. How one interprets 'the market', whether in the specific sense of the then Stock Exchange, or widely embracing financial affairs in general, I am uncertain. In the light of this opinion, however, advanced in November 1983, a Press revelation now exposes Barlow Clowes as an illegal trader, allegedly 'taking in millions of pounds from the public' during the subsequent two years. This was apparently because of an old exemption, by letter, from the necessity of licensing. To compound the confusion of the original exemption, in early

With an endless series of entanglements and
intrigues – open arrests, sentences . . .

1973, there was a DTI renewal of the company's licence in November 1987. And the more amazingly after their inspectors had begun an investigation prompted by widespread complaints and questionings.

Now we are finding ourselves involved not alone with the immediate past, but with an alarming tailback in unresolved fraud and financial mismanagement for which some are now being fished to the surface out of the murky depths. Satellite financial counsellors caught up, sometimes unwittingly, in the advocacy of over-ambitious income schemes ('We had our oldies . . . in British Government securities,' claimed one such steward, pathetically reassuring himself) are being suspended or closed down. Why? Because the SROs (Self Regulating Organisations) are scared out of their wits over the catalogue of disasters. But this is all closing the stable doors after the horses have bolted. I cannot see how it was remotely imagined that the rats, caught in the trap of encircling surveillance, would not somehow slither to the surface.

The bitter truth is that extreme restrictive pressures provoke risk-taking. Fund managers under the twin whips of competition and the need to out-perform may venture, short-term, heaven knows where, in what, in what size, and at what price? It is the same with the discarded Minimum Commission Scale pre-Bang: if you give stockbrokers the scope to undercut in expenses, in a desperate attempt to attract a popular turnover, you risk over-trading, over-committed resources, and the danger of collapse. A number of big market-makers attempted commission-cutting at the start, and inevitably retired seriously hurt. But they could stand the strain. Now, again, other expedients, such as tighter price-quotation spreads, are being introduced in an attempt by the market-makers to corner the dwindling business.

And what, out of all this, is the lesson for the reader? Refer back to my sub-section, 'Security, Risk, and Reward', in Chapter 4. I stress there that

... both a high return of income and scope for profit are inconsistent with first-class security.

I would now put it more directly:

> *Anybody or any firm dangling the bait of a much above average or over-exaggerated income return, or the apparent golden opportunity in any form, should be avoided like the plague.*

This should be the plaque above the bed.

In early September 1984, roughly paralleling the time I was writing my oft-quoted forecast about the likely unmarketability of shares in the lower post-Bang categories, the much respected and totally unbiased David Hopkinson, then chairman of the eminent M & G Investment Management Ltd, addressed a series of pertinent points to the Stock Exchange chairman, expressing his anxieties over the headlong flight to Big Bang. In particular he listed, most prophetically, five aspects of the then proposed measures following the abandonment of single capacity. These have since been proved most crucial. They were:

1. Markets should be conducted to protect both private and institutional investors from fraud and false prices.
2. The general public should have confidence in the efficiency and probity of the Stock Exchange.
3. The market should be organised to make it as simple as possible for smaller companies to raise new capital. It should also be organised to ensure sufficient market-makers so that liquidity in second, third and fourth line stocks does not dry up.
   (*This is the point I have continually been rubbing home for many years. – D.C.*)
4. The market should not be in such turmoil administratively that issues of Government stock and privatisation issues are damaged.
5. The market should not fall into the control of too few houses.

Stark now in the light of experience, a series of most valid points, most would agree. To them was added the back-ground ... 'For these reasons our view at M & G is that the Stock Exchange Council would be wise to proceed at a measured pace and should not be panicked either by the Government or the Bank of England or the powerful institu-tions into radical changes which would be difficult to reverse and to sort out if proved impractical in operation.'

Both in writing and lectures, albeit in slightly different terms, I was then expressing the same fears; and both of us, together with hundreds of highly experienced and articulate market authorities, have since been proved abundantly correct.

What now is the outcome of the specific points raised above? All are of proven importance, but perhaps the most important of all is the last ... *fear of the market falling into the control of too few houses* (I would have described, more pointedly, 'hands'). This fear has been importantly under-lined, almost as I write, by Stanislas Yassukovich, chairman of The Securities Association and also of Merrill Lynch Europe/ Middle East, in the third Patrick Hutber Memorial Lecture, delivered at Lloyd's of London on Thursday 21 July last.

Mr Yassukovich reinforced the opinions of Mr Hopkinson in asserting that:

The decline of the individual shareholder poses a threat to the free enterprise system and threatens also the long-term interests of those who manage and market collective investment schemes.

Here squarely was the 'too few houses' objection, because the speaker went on to explain how the decline of the individual saver as a direct participant in the equity market could be described a 'vicious circle'. The collective investment schemes, of whichever kind (soliciting funds from the savers for unit trusts or passively collecting for pension funds), would, in turn, themselves be influenced by the short-term comparative performance statistics. I took this argument to mean, in effect, that the investor at second hand would gravitate to the publicly proclaimed top performers, competitors (often the more prudent) would be drained of new funds, and thus the equity market would be compacted still further to the added detriment of the few dwindling individual investors. Hence the vicious circle of contraction. Because, in the end, the imperialistic few institutions remaining in play would no longer be able to take in each other's washing: if you know the other dealer's business, assuredly he knows yours.

If you finally kill off the individual private investor you threaten the entire free enterprise system; there must be the counterbalance of the private investor against the power of the institutional. That was Mr Yassukovich's main theme, elaborated, at least in part, by many of the points discussed above.

These points of view from several quarters complement, in a very real sense, what I have repeatedly written in the past, and certainly at length in the sixth chapter of this book – namely, that the stock market is fortunate regularly to deal for, and be advised and administered by, successive new generations of investors and attendant servicers. I earlier explained that were we to deal for an unchanging clientele which became with experience totally informed and disillusioned, then obviously everybody would know for certain what to do and act the same way; no opportunity would be afforded by the adoption of a contrary view, and *consequently no stock market*.

What, now, is the outcome in respect of the specific points raised above?

Although not unique in the history of world stock markets, the causes of Meltdown Monday (19 October 1987) will be long debated. Personally, I think this: in conditions already buoyant, and seen as likely to remain buoyant for many months on the burgeoning economic prospects, the market was let off the leash a year earlier in a climate of the unstoppable; greed knew no fear, optimism abounded, the

Government was intoxicated with its concept of a vast inter-national market in the City and well launched on its policy of successive privatisations; credit swept like chaff in the wind, and the big boys – the *really* Big Boys – were well in behind the UK's internationalism on a worldwide scale. These were the ingredients, and this roughly was the scenario of the launching pad for Big Bang. Others will fundamentally disagree.

But perhaps the most important underlying factor was the inexperience of the new 'talents' embraced by this great financial get-together ... the striving entrepreneurs, the skaters on remarkably thin ice, the take-over wizards, the analytical genies, the jugglers, the gurus – an inconceivable gathering. These 'professionals' (who said it and from whence were they dredged up?) were paid obscene salaries, and became known as 'yuppies', who distorted the lifestyle wherever they went. They also succeeded in misdirecting thousands of innocents embarking on the money trail, and severely denting many employers for whom they toiled.

As I write, the new intake is being disbanded in double quick time from merchant bankers and manipulative mammoths of all kinds, American, British, and dubiously elsewhere. The chief economist of a major stockbroker suggests that the ultimate toll in City redundancies could total 50,000. 'In the build-up to Big Bang,' he explained, 'everyone was spending money trying to gain a presence.' Countless thousands of pounds and dollars have been lost in this excursion.

It is a highly cynical reflection that this Government's Big Bang, with all its showy pretensions and pious platitudes about a new morality in money management, should have turned out such a colossal backfire. The acclaimed era of vastly cheap dealing for the small investor (remember, 'shop around'!), electronically slick documentation, freedom of choice among a prolificity of market-makers stripped of all the stultifying rules of a Victorian museum-piece.

[98]

Yet with all these widely advertised advantages, where in under a year did they get us? With grotesquely higher dealing costs (except for the institutional dealers), massive delays in processing bargains, rampant 'insider' trading and multiple fraud, the faces of the eminent and supposedly trustworthy besmeared with the egg of corruption, and the emasculation of the ancient market-place replaced by a so-called 'service' culminating in the slapping down of the telephone in termi- nation of the small person's first humble, stumbling words of approach. All the unhappy consequences suspected in those so timely words of warning . . . 'It [the stock market] should be organised . . . so that liquidity in second, third and fourth line stocks does not dry up.'

Here, in the beckoning beacons I have outlined, was the 'money trail' on which the small investor, prime target of those who echoed 'wider share ownership', 'individual share ownership', were led forth into the promised land. But the conception, repeatedly massaged, that stocks and shares were not the preserve of the privileged few has been proved a mirage. The public has little confidence in the market in its new computerised form. The administrative background is in turmoil, and the new market-makers tend to deal on a 'pick- 'n'-mix' basis, favouring those shares which are the best 'trades' at the given moment; jettisoning those less promising for their own 'books'. I am aware that the market-makers must quote prices in the securities they have accepted to deal in, but I am referring here to the degree of attention applied to the focal shares as distinct from the non-runners.

10

RUMOUR RUNS RIFE

'Silly Season'

July to mid-August is customarily known in the stock market as the 'silly season' . . . the dog-days of the holiday exodus and its distractions. Business then dries up, and the few professionals around are desperate to dredge some turnover out of the torpor. It is then you may expect the rumourers to start priming the pump, not necessarily as originators of enticing tales (difficult to identify), but certainly as ready recipients and elaborators of such persuasive items going the rounds. Notoriously communicative, the City grapevine travels far and wide.

Most of these rumours will circulate around popularly identified takeover targets and the colourful alleged predators invariably identified – by the Press, at least – as stalking this field. This kind of gossip is of abiding interest in these acquisitive times of international fingers in the fruity pies and frothy brews. As with our High Street retail chains, with their billions in eye-catching property, the shares can quickly be stampeded, if often but briefly, by a speculative following for an arresting buzz about astronomic break-up value ('cash-rich' an enticing term) or the rumour that a near 5% equity stake has adroitly changed hands. Spectacular turnover in targeted alpha stocks is another bait unlikely to go unheeded.

And at this high season the market-makers are usually ill-stocked with available shares supplies in these popular categories, and quick to mark up prices well out of reach – as equally quick to mark them down again. Underlying technical strength is enhanced by the fact that the big institutional holders are generally reluctant sellers into the suspected autumn rise.

Another point. Equities like these, which conform adroitly to the ebb and flow within the popular sights, are unlikely to lead the modest aspirant permanently astray; although the venture may initially misfire, then, almost odds on, there will come a renewed outburst and the chance to exit. The only requirement is the financial ability to adopt the commitment short-term. This remains true, except in the case of one of the prima donnas of the takeover stage when it may be advisable to look further ahead.

About financing a short-term venture of this type at the 'silly season' stage, this may seem totally at variance with what I have regularly advised, and re-emphasise here in my concluding chapter, 'Tenets on the Money Trail' – namely, that a share bought purposely as an Account speculation should not, if it fails to perform, be adopted belatedly as an 'investment'. But the cases are not parallel: the potential 'lift' in a continually argued takeover stock will, likely as not, enable the purchaser to extricate himself; good as it may be intrinsically, the minor equity that misfires lacks the regular ebb and flow, and may well confine the purchaser for an indefinite time.

The Bleak, Black Bottom

Because, as already stressed, it is easy to make money on a consistent rise, as equally to lose it on a fall, perhaps the most useful point to consider in the stock market cycle is the bleak, black bottom of the pit – if you can determine where that lies. I refer figuratively.

Indeed, many may wonder whether anything will remotely ever return. To restore your confidence, and as an instructive illustration, remember that at the nadir of the collapse in early 1975, when the fringe banks and fleeting financiers were caught perilously between the twin fires of short borrowing and long lending, and the *Financial Times* 30-share index slumped to a twenty-year 'low' of 146.0, shares were, as earlier described, literally given away.

Was everybody raving mad? No. In this wild distortion of prices, with the professionally destructive 'bears' fanning the flames with false rumours, the great Burmah Oil, no less, were ruthlessly raided down to around 19p. This slightly freakish showing was due both to Burmah's cash débâcle and to the weighing factor of the equally raided Bowater paper giant. When I then queried of a dealer-friend, was it not the golden opportunity to step in with both feet? he replied, in horror, 'Donald, you wouldn't if you were actually here! You don't realise what things are like! Burmah may crash any moment!'

In the bars across the Street the talk was of imminent financial armageddon.

Then, virtually within a few days, like a child who momentarily cries from a tumble on the pavement, it was all smiles again, and prices soared. Of course, it was a violent mark-up in prices by the then jobbers. It is always a question of which moves the fastest: the market-makers' pencils or the buyers' orders through the system. Obviously the former in anticipation. Unfortunately the rigmarole surrounding modern dealing practice places the individual investor at an increasing disadvantage. The more he is 'protected', the more the chance of successful – which means speedy – dealing is inhibited by kindness. But here lies the great truism that it is a matter of personal opinion whether share prices are viewed too outrageously high or too abysmally low. Such judgement is the province of every investor as well as every market-maker. Here, truly perhaps, the 'golden opportunity' to which we so hopefully refer!

By about mid-that-March, the index had crashed up through the 300 barrier, thus more than doubling from the bottom. Of interest perhaps to students of Chartlaw, between November '74, when a rally occurred into the 170-odd area, and the mid-January '75 revival, the market described the classic bottoming-out formation – the 'reverse head-and-shoulders' (roughly a 'w' with arms extended).

Purposefully Pessimistic

Market rumour is adapted to the conditions, is often highly contagious; false rumour the more so, particularly when prices are crumbling like shifting shale, and it is easy for the purposefully pessimistic to destroy a well-warranted share. Slump is no respecter of real value; nor boom its perceptive assessor. Nonsenses are created in both directions. And as just stressed, these are when those 'golden opportunities' are perhaps presented – for buying or selling.

Around the time of which I am writing, the unlikely duo of Harold Wilson and Enoch Powell united in mutual condemnation of the wilful destructionists then in our midst. The former spoke contemptuously, I recall, of the 'weevils' in the market-place, continually gnawing at the fabric of share prices by 'short' selling; the latter rounded on the gloomsters, whose chorus of woe was aimed at knocking the heart and soul out of the market. This was only shortly after the National Westminster Bank's shares were wantonly raided on rumours that it had received large-scale support from the Bank of England, partly because of its involvement with British Land. This story was, of course, immediately and roundly denied. British Land were themselves then destroyed to well under 20p on rumours of virtual bankruptcy.

In my last article for Patrick Hutber, a sort of valedictory piece in the *Sunday Telegraph* of 29 September 1974, I concluded on the same theme of false rumour, writing that . . .

> *Those who would redeem the old status of the Stock Exchange talk ambiguously about the need of a new, acceptable image, as if by affixing a label of quality, this could be imparted conveniently by the institution as such.*
>
> *On the contrary, the process of redemption, as in the deliberate trafficking in destructive rumour, cannot be wished down from above; it must spring from the grass roots of the market-place itself in recognition of the responsibilities of the practitioner both to the investor and the nation.*

So here is the point of which the newcomer must be wary – the spread of false rumour, as alarmist on the downside as it is persuasive on the up.

Technique of the Takeover

Having suggested the takeover as being the most likely diversion during the slumbrous midsummer days, it might be as well to discuss briefly what the technique of a company acquisition – call it merger, uncalled-for bid, or direct pillaging – involves.

As to the background, the takeover of one company by another has been a continuing feature of the post Second World War trend. They commenced quietly enough, and logically, with the acquisition, generally for reason of valuable property sites ripe for redevelopment, of companies outdated by circumstances. As a typical example, the old drapers' warehousemen. As the small, independent draper was ousted by the multiple stores, the trading of the great Victorian institu-

*As the small, independent draper was ousted by
the multiples stores*

tions such as Cook Son & Co. (St Paul's) gradually died. In turn, a long succession of textile producers, particularly in cottons, were absorbed, merged and 'rationalised'. All this began inconspicuously at first, in the late 40s. Into the 50s, the pace quickened with excursions into popular catering, into food production/distribution, and into the drinks industry (soft and hard), notably the mopping up or 'umbrellaing' of smaller breweries, all aimed protectively at bigger and more monopolistic groupings.

For the whole of this trend, which has steadily gained momentum over the years, one can look again to the growth of institutional participation in the industrial equity parallel with the declining influence of the individual investor. The continual channelling of funds into the major shares not only created in its flow a scarcity value in the shares concerned, but steadily intensified that scarcity by establishing a well-informed 'lead' to desirable shares for the investor at large. Ironically, as a result, the smaller companies were retarded in growth because new finance was not so readily accessible, a restrictive influence rendering many the more vulnerable to absorption on beggarly terms. A contributory reason for the then concentration on the 'big' equities was the background threat of Socialist nationalisation: hoist the prices high, outpace the assets value, it was argued, to erect a high protective barrier.

Then, entering the 60s, the acquisitive turned to the cash-replete company looked on as what is often termed a 'shell' – a conveniently ready-made (and thereby cheap) corporate structure for the insertion of a totally different, more lucrative, business. Into this category fell a number of Sri Lanka (Ceylon that was) rubber companies that had accumulated cash due to uninterrupted production during the Second World War (the territory was not occupied). Remember Bukit Lintang, to re-emerge as a placing in early 1959 in the reconstructed form of Lintang Investments, under the Maxwell Joseph banner. It was the receptacle of the posh Dolphin Square flats-swimming-pool-catering complex.

Under the impact of this gathering spate of bids, buy-outs, and get-togethers, the Stock Exchange list of officially quoted capital issues steadily narrowed from its original 9,500-odd, and that despite many new share appearances. Whether or not because of the undignified spectacles in Throgmorton Street occasioned by the share placings of the late 50s, it is perhaps more than a coincidence that the City's Panel on Take-Overs and Mergers was formulated in 1959 on the initiative of the Governor of the Bank of England. A working party was then set up comprising representatives of all the relevant financial groupings, to consider good business practice in the conduct of takeovers and mergers. Basically the purpose of the Panel is to administer the non-statutory City Code in interpretation of the collective opinion of all concerned, so as to ensure equality in the dissemination of company news, and the opportunity for action, as affecting the shares of an offeror or offeree company, thereby eliminating as far as possible privileged information to the possible advantage of the 'inside' trader.

'Asset-strippers' of the 60s

The mechanism of adequate control was not really in place to curb the brazen exploits of the new generation of entrepreneurs emerging in the 60s. Then the takeovers were mounted for (impolitely) 'asset-stripping'; (more politely) 'putting under-utilised assets to work more effectively'. Then a large number of small industrial concerns still in independent business had been content for years to rest on such laurels as their ageing directors conceived; their share prices drifted insidiously downwards, hugely exposing underlying assets value. The attention of the asset-strippers was tacitly invited. Who could really blame them? Background and associated interests, such as the old Yorkshire Brick's valuable silica sand deposits, were quickly ferreted out.

The asset-stripper's ideal formula was a small issued equity capital capable of being blown up like a balloon by successive scrip bonusing; and a sizeable and readily encashable fixed asset in some form of property, preferably bricks and mortar. This combination imparted the essential gearing, and a plausible story acceptable to most, that the assets would be 'put to work', if hopelessly watered in the process. Up temporarily went the profits as released cash was redeployed in the purchase of higher earnings; up too went the old, modest issued capital, in line with the new-found 'growth', by way of a one-for-one in new free shares. Naturally the main architects, retaining a large chunk of the originally acquired shares, did very nicely, thank you, while the balloon flew away even higher – until it burst. For later followers, it was a case of now you see it, now you don't! These times, in stark contrast, big businesses are bought out for their patents and market share, and conceivably to eliminate competition. This is one stage more blatant than the once despised asset-strippers.

The 'Concert Party'

The newcomer may or may not have heard of what is known in the City vernacular as a 'concert party'. It has nothing to do with pierrots on the sands. About it, I should stress, there are two definitions – that of Section 204 of the Companies Act 1985, and that of the City's Take-Over Panel, of which it is nowadays one of the latter's main preoccupations. A 'concert party' is a means by which a coterie of friends or firms or both may – I stress, *may* – connive together in the individual purchases (and 'warehousing') of a particular ordinary share for the purpose of an eventual predator parcelling the lot together to mount the takeover of an unsuspecting victim. In fact, today the victim cannot be wholly unsuspecting, because the accumulation of over 4.9% of a company's issued equity capital, whether voting or non-voting, requires the immediate declaration of such interest to the company concerned, and the subsequent reporting of each full point change in such holding, whether up or down. The obligations of the creditor are now to be tightened further.

The problem in describing the 'concert party' is that if one gives a potted version (as I have, picturesquely, above), then everybody is left with a shadowy impression; yet, if one attempts to be really explanatory, then the risk is a novel. As explained in an important judgement on a case of precisely this nature, the Panel (incidentally an adjunct of the former Stock Exchange) exercises a self-imposed task in regulating and policing the conduct of takeovers and mergers in the financial market in the UK. As distinct from this, the Companies Act 1985 sets out the statutory provisions to justify, if necessary, the intervention of the Court.

Without being lured into the complexities of the various stop-go levels in the percentage of a targeted company's equity capital which may be acquired before decisive action is obligatory on the part of an accumulator of such shares, the attainment of 30% is the point at which an open bid must be made to all equity holders. And this at the highest price the bidder has paid during the ensuing twelvemonth. Which explains why so many pointed accumulations are adroitly halted just short of 30%. Instructive cases for the beginner to contemplate, because with the alternative possibility of rival bids, the initial accumulator will undoubtedly look for a profit.

It might be appropriate to add here that takeover bids came under a two-pronged attack in parallel articles in the mid-summer issue of *Crossbow*, the voicepiece of the Conservative Bow Group. First, Mr Rodney Atkinson was highly critical of the way the Government agencies ignored the regional dimension in refusing to refer the Nestlé and Suchards bids for Rowntrees to the Monopolies Commission. Bids with a strong regional aspect did harm, he argued, to the local economy by a permanent loss of jobs in services as well as in the target company.

More pointed perhaps was the view of Mr Simon Blunt, that the City acts as a lobby for *laissez-faire* policy because the fees and profits from the takeover industry are increasingly vital to its success. *'The benefits to the City of takeover activities are self-evident – in fact, they appear to be almost the lifeblood of the City today.'* This valid criticism links back to the short-termism to which I, and so many other observers, have more recently emphasised. As Mr Blunt advises, there is a need to reduce the power of the market raiders and arbitrageurs in promoting bids. I could not more heartily agree.

11

GENUS OF THE ANALYTICAL GURU

Alarmingly accelerated since Big Bang, there has grown up this decade a species of specialist adviser nurtured and paraded in the ranks of the banking-market-making conglomerates.

There has grown up parallel with these a new species of financial scribe who is limited in the matter of essential background, has an inflated opinion of everything within his/her orbit, and seems to rely conveniently for material on probings among the institutional planters of such seeds as may need fertilising. This provides the aura of the big-name sources. At least, so it must be imagined, because most of the market commentaries in the better-class newspapers are punctuated with the names of analysts and so-called experts, not only usefully advertising themselves, but with even greater publicity accorded the stables for which they work.

I am actually reading two such commentary pieces as I write, and noting the reference to so-and-so, 'the City drinks guru', what's-it's 'analysts reckon that . . .', and more of the same. The beauty of this specious style of copy, easily garnered over the telephone, is that should it go the wrong way, the blame can be shuffled back to source. After all, it was an impeccable quarter to quote! And the mouthpiece can equally disclaim that he knew he was being reported, well knowing that undoubtedly he would be. The truth is that the former share selector, writing on his own original research, is now too nervous of advancing beyond platitudes on what is already positively known from the companies concerned or what is digested and packaged for them for the banker-broker mouthpieces. The Press, except for certain publications with absolute clearance from the Securities and Investments Board, certainly appears reluctant to venture much resembling the old forthright 'tip' (this one a 'Buy') because of the possible liability under the Financial Services Act. Some may have noticed how the previous pertinent points offered in the Sunday columns escape neatly beneath the umbrella of some institutional analyst's assessment. The handling of readers' direct share inquiries seems mostly to have ended.

Acknowledging that the quite extensive financial coverage of the responsible newspapers has for long been a source of useful leads to promising, or at least potentially interesting, shares, now that this guidance is smothered by the wet blankets of enforced discretion the would-be investor of limited means is largely denied resort to straightforward recommendations. The hundred-thousand-plus portfolio may of itself command attention. But the much smaller investor, seeking real supervision, may be steered politely aside with an escapist letter suggesting the submergence of the client's capital in the broker's unit trust department. There the handling may be on a wholly discretionary basis, and the degree of impersonality may be judged from the fact that one is often asked to agree to averaged dealing prices which could be better – or worse – than operating independently. In other words, the client's business is merged in bulk dealings.

With the polite but scarcely informative letter will probably come a glossy, explanatory brochure, for the intending investor's signature and return, plus cheque if it is intended to proceed. The many clauses in the typed submission seem, from those I have read, to let the broker out of a few tight corners should he put a foot wrong. On the other hand, the bounty offered seems expected to be taken largely on trust by the client.

This is the very factual projection of the conclusion with which I ended my last paperback. Over two years ago now, I wrote the following:

> *For their own convenience and the greater economy of their operations, not to say bolster their own selections, the institutions and the broker-cum-banker conglomerates want total command over packaged schemes of investment. 'Use our expertise,' they invite. 'Trouble-free investment . . . ?'*
> *Another version of Big Brother!*

Circle of Make-belief

To revert to my opening theme, the types I pinpointed there – the new-style financial analysts and journalists – are often the products of that similarly post-war breed – the personnel/ executive selectionists without whose declared expertise the business-person has been persuaded they cannot exist. Thus the blind lead the blind, because the miracle-makers them-selves know little of the history, background and intricacies of the securities business. Translate this truth still wider: the whole structure of the International Stock Exchange is diluted with outsiders who know little about the inner workings of the market-place.

However, I often feel that this nicely rounded circle of much make-belief, this slap-me-on-the-back, mutual admira-tion society, has been developed on the theory of Parkin-son's law of work expansion to fill available time. But taken to the extreme of creating little private cliques of often grossly overpaid persons to do jobs for which they get exaggerated credence can be dangerous. Consider, aside, many of the Inner London councils.

Nowadays opinion and hearsay are so persuasively dressed up as to masquerade as fact. By way of factory visits, actuarial investigations by teams of brokers' economists, predictions are often so miraculously accurate as virtually to complement eventual results. One regularly reads of a company's prestigious brokers seemingly dotting the 'i's' of their client's profits forecast. Indeed, one wonders whether it is not the old begrudged 'insider information'? It has been admitted to me . . . 'A grey area.'

To pursue the same argument, if small parties of highly interpretative analysts are regularly made privy to companies' developments, trading trends and prospects (obviously to the extent only that it is decided to drop such information), how does one distinguish these privileged insights from the barside blonde who, in the rosy light of dawn, picks up a little gem of indiscretion from a besotted chairman? More pertinent, how are such analysts' private gleanings used prior to general dissemination? Certainly the fund manipulators do not pay the piper to enliven the steps of Mr and Mrs Average. Yet it may be observed from a study of the financial commentaries on the opinions and revelations of these sources, that big price movements are often sprung in the shares of the companies sponsoring these happy gatherings – or, as the papers now refer to them, 'presentations'. Certainly if there are any beneficiaries, the ordinary investor is not the recipient of the first droppings from the tree of knowledge.

The old, scornful City aside, 'Where there's a tip there's a tap!' is as valid today as ever it was. So, to the small investor, I would suggest always looking the gift horse squarely in the mouth. I have become exhausted by too many mounts. The second truth is that 'inside' information is something for which, should you use it and make a profit, you could technically go to gaol; but should you make a loss, you will certainly receive no strawberries.

Virtually synonymous with the subject of the previous

*'Inside' information . . . should you use it and
make a profit, you could technically go to gaol*

chapter, 'Rumour Runs Rife', and the shadowy, often undetectable, 'insider' trading, are the subjects of 'Chinese Walls' and the frequent 'leaks' of price-sensitive information between, around, and far beyond these cosmetic erections. About all these interrelated matters the venturer on the money trail should be in no doubt. It will be appreciated that, after all, almost any important company development, impending takeover, profits surge, new issue, or proposed major acquisition will be signalled and ventilated in advance: as already indicated, the particular company's broker will be apprised of the event and will prepare the ground. Such usually leads to an anticipatory flutter in the share price. The shareholder will appreciate that the movement, up or down, may be ultimately for the right reason, but as quickly contradicted in the short. Particularly in 'thin' markets, do not necessarily rush in to conform with snap price reactions.

The Ethical Divide

The Chinese Walls have no substance; it is a phrase to describe the ethical divide between those privy to corporate information in the analytical department of the financial conglomerate, and their share-dealing/market-making colleagues on the other side, to whom such information is supposedly beyond the pale. The intention is clinically clear enough; equally clear is that such sublime faith is misplaced. In the hot summer days, youths quaff their pints on the City pavements, talking to distraction. Apart from girls, parties, and Porsches, of what do they talk? Not always of their dockland window-boxes, for certain. This is well known from the succession of recent leaks.

It has more than once been suggested that a benevolent blind eye even now tends to be turned to the occasional impropriety, the leak, the slip of the tongue, the sagacious nod or wink. In the past, it is claimed, the dropped hint was countenanced to help what is euphemistically called an 'orderly market'; to ensure that the surprise result or development did not hit the market with such force as to catch the professionals seriously on the wrong foot, thus disrupting the whole price structure.

It is true that news and events of this magnitude may have been judiciously 'sensed' by the old market . . . to put it no stronger, in order to iron out sudden shocks to the system. At the same time, dual capacity, with its isolation of the client's agent (the stockbroker) from the self-motivated market-maker (the jobber), placed the potential business on both sides in reasonably watertight compartments. Both practitioners sought to execute their business on best terms, and the basis of such endeavour was to keep it close to the chest, for the broker certainly without revealing his dealing intention. To be caught quizzing over an opposite number's 'book' would not have endeared one to the opposition. Now the electronic screens tell all at a glance; there is little or no chance of serious bargaining, in fact to do so in number could spoil one's market. The investor is confronted with a bland, unresponsive dealing machine.

The old-time jobbers, who were in competition among themselves and would originally have numbered a dozen or more in a share like Courtaulds, were certainly not disclosers to the brokers. The only occasions on which the two sides would open up would be when, because of size (say, a quarter of a million XYZs), it was obviously prudent to leave the business firm with a single big jobber for execution in his own time. The presence of any such big order would be treated with discretion by the recipient jobber, who naturally would not want to spoil his chances of doing the business. Equally, a broker would undercut his own market were he to hawk such an order around.

'Tip of the Iceberg?' Probably Not

All of which is not to suggest, by comparison, that insider trading on leaked information, wholesale penetration of Chinese Walls, is more prevalent today; people who declare, suspiciously, 'Oh, the tip of the iceberg?' are ignorant of the facts. The truth is that what comes often dramatically to light are the isolated cases. It is probably true to suggest that a number of the instances of the use of inside information uncovered are not pursued, the culprits being too small and inept to warrant further investigation. In fact, if they were, it is doubtful now whether the investigative machine would be adequate to handle the weight of inquiry. The preoccupation is with the serious cases. *Which is by no means to suggest that the rest have not been pinpointed and can continue to overplay their hands with impunity. Let them be warned: they can't.*

12

TENETS ON THE
MONEY TRAIL

I know I am now re-potting, in slightly richer compost, what I have already tried to plant in your minds, but I want, in conclusion, to underline the main points – and pointers – of practice regularly applicable, as I have known, over the decades.

*　　*　　*

Stock markets – all markets – are motivated by the counterplay of the rival emotions of greed and fear. Both well demonstrated in the film *Wall Street*. When people are more greedy than fearful, prices go up; when fear predominates, prices go down. And the great deception lies in the fact that both emotions are self-generating: optimism proliferates with success; pessimism perpetuates failure. Which is precisely why the investor at large so often misjudges the crucial turning points in the market's overall cycles.

*　　*　　*

Timing is all-important. It is first, second, third, and finally of prime importance. You can buy analytically the best share in the market, the ultimate pearl of wisdom, but you will not necessarily be preserved from loss in an overall fall if you buy it at fundamentally the wrong time. As many investment portfolios are marred by the right shares bought at the wrong time, as by any old shares bought at any time.

*   *   *

Do not be deluded that a rise is to eternity. The successful investor consolidates his wealth by selling too soon, on the principle of letting the other man 'have a bit'.

*   *   *

There is an old sarcasm that 'an investor is a disappointed speculator'. Meaning that should you buy a share purposely as an Account speculation, and the speculation misfires, don't adopt it as an 'investment'. That is the way to disaster – the ultimate rag-bag of also-rans. It is essential not to become bogged down among non-runners, and consequently lose the initiative. With Timing and Imagination, Initiative is the third prong of successful attack. When the outcome is success, it is called, politely, vision; when failure, the victim is disparagingly dismissed as having reached impossibly for the stars.

*   *   *

There is no profit in the past, as such; it is of value only in so far as it can point the future. By this, I mean that a study of, say, the cyclical record of a particular industry may suggest its likely performance in the future or, in the case of an individual company, much may often be learned about such matters as future dividend policy from the proportion of earnings customarily disbursed and the ratio preserved between interim and final dividend rates. To this extent, the thoughtful investor refers constantly to the background record for guidance ahead.

*   *   *

[120]

Many investors buy the past as a matter of prudence. They feel it better to be safe than sorry; they are influenced by good results and an increased dividend into believing the shares of a particular company a 'good buy'. By all the statistical yardsticks, they may indeed be intrinsically fair value. Yet what the newcomer may tend to overlook is that, at the full-blown stage of the year-end results, the position is over-exposed marketwise; and with another half-year to run before the interim results, the chances are that the shares will drift sideways.

*   *   *

In winning or inheriting money, being possessed for the first time of the necessary wherewithal, do not be too anxious to be the recipient of your first contract note. Think well before you move. Coincidentally, almost as I type these words, a correspondent in the *Financial Times* similarly states that the investor 'must accord the preservation of capital a higher priority than the maximisation of potential returns'. How true.

*   *   *

No bell tolls resoundingly to warn of the market's main pivot-ings. On the contrary, one may have to strain for the tinkling of seeming trivialities which, spreading in a chain reaction, can often point the way.

*   *   *

Remember, at the bottom of every slump lie the bare bones of the next boom. They only wait to be clad by the new circum-stances from which will be argued afresh solutions to the old, old, but eternally fascinating, problem of how to make

[121]

money in stocks and shares. Be assured, some genius will resurrect them!

*　　　*　　　*

Uncertainty often points the takeover trail as the best to follow. Well signposted by professional buying, as potential bidders and their satellites stake or extend their initial claims, the novice follower is generally assured some sort of springboard in the event of a temporary slip in such shares.

*　　　*　　　*

In narrow, almost pre-determined stock markets, against a background of acute stock shortage, situation shares can move fast – for a time. The professional operators, fund managers and the like may virtually write their own meal tickets by reason of the following they generate when so few market leads are available to the public. What moves in relative isolation attracts attention.

*　　　*　　　*

But sporadic speculative activity is extremely shallow. Specialities are not promoted for the benefit of the bandwagoners prepared to mount any moving vehicle oblivious of the facts. It is generally, indeed, when the public is providing the final propulsion that the in-traders, entrenched in the lower price range, are adroitly vacating their seats.

*　　　*　　　*

Assets are the quest of the big professional financiers – assets and what is known as 'market share', trade names and old-established sales outlets. It can pay to follow the buying when their hand is shown, but make sure that these assets are under-represented in the share prices. 'Play the players' is often sound advice.

*   *   *

It is a cynical reflection that whereas takeovers were formerly the penalty of bad management, they are now the directorial distraction of good. They also impose the necessity of costly defence. Such intrusive attentions suggest that the shareholder should look long and carefully before accepting the dangled carrot of the boarder. If a situation is so tempting as to attract one aspirant to control, it will probably attract competitors. Opportunists seldom venture costly involvements for nothing, albeit a stake may sometimes be adopted in the belief of an ensuing auction and resultant quick profit for those hung in on the sidelines. For the entrepreneur, in fact, stake-building in likely takeover situations often provides an attractive two-way bet.

*   *   *

You may wonder how an unsuccessful takeover bid can possibly be helpful to shareholders in the intended victim? It may well because, in order to justify their case against acquisition, the directors will have had to disclose previously hidden financial strength. For example, freehold property could have been undervalued in the balance-sheet. In any case, a previously unenterprising management is probably given a spur resulting in greater efficiency, a more economic use of assets, and eventually higher profits and dividends. To this extent, many an unsuccessful takeover attempt has not only put up – but kept up – the shares concerned.

*   *   *

Consideration of the technical position in a share is always important, but bear in mind that it may not invariably mean what it seems. It may not necessarily parallel the company's financial and industrial position; it could well falsify the price of a particular share or group of shares. There are instances of shares quoted patently too high – or low; and they may continue to be so, for the very reason that the falsification is widely acknowledged on a 'bear' – or 'bull' – position already built in. Infinitesimal yield and other adverse fundamentals are often ineffectual in quickly redressing such price anomalies.

*   *   *

What can be deceptive about the stock market, on a wholly short-term basis, is that it is often technically strongest when prices are sliding, and the reverse. This is because the big institutional operators are more generally present in the background when lines of stock are on offer. In effect, they buy when they are best able, often resting inconspicuously just beneath the surface of the market.

*   *   *

Looked at from a slightly different angle, apart from other factors, the technical position is important because either an over-bought or an over-sold position, as a consequence of too many people discounting ahead of events, can falsify the effect of good or bad results in the short run. This is especially true of companies overcome by serious difficulties, in whose shares a substantial 'bear' structure exists. Then one may find that, instead of going down, the price may, for a time, go up.

*   *   *

Naturally the ordinary investor will find it difficult to determine whether the market position in a particular share is especially refined or underlined by special pressures. The price trend and the presence of regular option dealers may give some indication. As a very rough rule, however, a share is least likely to be influenced by anticipatory business at the company's 'off-season' periods, midway between dividend and profit announcements.

*　　*　　*

The 'technical position', to which I keep referring, is the availability or otherwise of share supplies, the underlying trend which often, as described above, defies the surface flurries; and the indefinable 'feel' of the market. This last is not something which can be taught. It is variously described by charts and indices, more often sensed from long experience.

*　　*　　*

In barren markets, those who try to beat the vagaries of the trend run quite unwarranted risks. Business is too transparently 'thin', their trades often too precise in size and timing, not to shriek attention. At times like these the market is fully prepared to adjust quotations down quite ruthlessly until equilibrium is restored. Prices are slashed out of all proportion to the volume of selling. The result of such refinement is that when buyers do appear they find little or no stock available . . . at least, not at yesterday's prices on which, perversely, everyone wants to deal. Another justification for the old adage – *deal when you can*. Technically, this is the point at which the upside scope is greater than the downside risk.

*　　*　　*

Technically, too, the fundamental difference between the position now and that obtaining in 1939 is that then there was

*The wonder share of today may so easily become
the waste paper of tomorrow!*

largely a buyer's market for shares. The old-time operators had the saying, 'Shares are made to sell.' This meant that, in conditions generally of deflation and stable money, they recognised the need to 'push' their wares and rapidly to convert colourful pieces of paper (the then share certificates) into cash. The less scrupulous were consequently known as 'share-pushers'. Nowadays, conversely, the urgency is to convert depreciating cash into the offset of physical assets.

*   *   *

With the latest pressures for high propriety, protection of capital is necessarily always the more immediate aim of market advisers than the gain of more, with the result that every development at home and abroad is scanned for its hidden bogy. With such vigilance for the worst, market opinion must, on occasions, hit the nail on the head. But, unhappily, favourable points are not accorded such ready credence, and their truth, often clear as crystal to the detached observer, takes time in struggling to general acceptance through a destructive fog of doubts and fears.

*   *   *

Consider again; when the storm has spent its force, and the market is just stirring up from the bottom, the established shareholder would be advised to take account of the detracting influence of a stale 'bull' position. The symptoms then are just the same as at the peak – pitifully low business volume, irregular movements as shares drag along in a rut of profound uncertainty. The private investor, overtaken by calamity he was too late in acknowledging, is belatedly taking advantage of the first upturn to scurry out when, in fact, he would be best advised to sit very tight. It is then that the long-headed are quietly tucking away bargain stock. The new buyer would be wise to apply a little of that psychology of which I wrote in my opening, and not be deterred by the selling of tired, dispirited holders in the early stages of revivals.

*   *   *

To recapitulate with punch lines:

Few outsiders can consistently make money by trading in shares. Be an investor rather than a trader.

Do not become hypnotised by the chart signals, up or down, but try rather to calculate what others believe such signals to portend.

Think long and well before you move.

Beware of any big build-up towards an established market milestone, such as the Budget or an important dividend declaration. Its passing may well present a void.

Finally, never forget that the wonder share of today may so easily become the waste paper of tomorrow!

13

WHY SUCH A RESOUNDING BANG?

Commenting on market-makers' desperate attempts to get on terms with collapsed business, by narrowing their dealing spreads, one un-named broker is reputed to have made the bald observation: '*The system does not work as it is and they are just making things worse.*' Which politely summarises what many might say about Big Bang having led the old-style British investor into a labyrinth of inconceivable bewilderment compared with anything to which they were previously accustomed.

And what, in the end, were the young scribblers, those hyped into the market-making conglomerates for the glittering prizes, expected to say . . . gleefully. 'Look, no hands!' as the market slithered to disaster?

Our investor, who, right throughout the Victorian, Edwardian, and George the Fifthian eras, had been on the old school tie-up with his literally neighbouring stockbroker, suddenly found himself rudely discarded to the tail-end of the queue, a supplicant at the table of the brash, American-style, computerised automatons . . . could anybody really have conceived that these totally square pegs could be accommodated in the contra-shaped holes provided in the new set-up? But incredibly they did.

Yet once, and not so long ago on my recollection, the Stock

Exchange was a convivial club. Which was anathema to the Press and left-wing circles, particularly the alleged high selectivity in the matter of new members, although little of that was evident with the post-war intake during the late 60s. One irrepressible contributor to the Aussie nickel boom in 1968 hardly distinguished himself, as subsequent history relates.

Then, except for the manager of the Mutual Reference Society, and possibly the personal secretaries of a few of the most eminent persons (the Chairman, naturally), there were few, if any, women on the administrative staff. This was, in any case, constituted somewhat on the 'two-man-and-a-boy' principle. Everybody knew everybody else, and if one wanted anything – say, to gently twist an arm – one just drifted around among departmental heads and secretaries and amicably made one's mark. Long before there was an official Public Relations Committee, set up with its corresponding Department in the 50s, I was frequently delegated to contribute my speaking and scribbling efforts in an unofficial capacity. Strangely, departmental minions still occasionally ring me up today to dot an 'i' about some way-back fact or figure. Happily, in the days of which I write, it was not suspected that you secreted a bomb about your person.

There was a sedate, panelled library on the second floor where slumbrous members reposed in deep leather armchairs beneath copies of *The Statist*; and where others, completely lacking in office accommodation, repaired to do their documentary work. The old-time jobbers, a few running eccentric one-man bands, carved themselves if not hugely lucrative, at least sustainable little niches specialising in the most remote obscurities. Occasionally sought for their wares, these could be unearthed from nooks and crannies on the seats surrounding the great, marble-faced pillars that interrupted the 'floor' area. They had to be roused from dusty hibernation, laboriously to look up the price – an often inordinately wide one – in some near-abandoned preference share. But all done with the most supreme courtesy.

Unlike conditions today, under the more widely constituted Council of the International Stock Exchange, the long-ago Committee for General Purposes, which governed with an iron hand the conduct of the member and his dealing practices, would still countenance with kindly patronage and sufferance the most extraordinary extroverts and oddities. Young men about today think themselves of the same ilk, but let me assure them that they are nothing of the kind. What I have for years written about, in description of the market's past and its personalities, is the ungarnished truth. But so extravagant, it seems, in the present context, that few will believe it.

The total severance by Big Bang from this cosy backwater conveniently enabled the constraint or even displacement of members who had long been conceived as thorns in the administrative flesh. Unless they or their firms had been seriously in breach of the rules, the annual re-election of members was virtually rubber-stamped. But with the world trampling in by the front door, here certainly was an opportunity to show any objectors the back. Or am I suspicious? Yet the fact of some delay in granting a few of the smaller broking firms full authorisation under the Financial Services Act may be due in part to some questionings over the past.

Pace of the Slowest

At the same time, I suspect it was due to solicitude for the conservatism of the elderly membership by the all-embracing Councils which replaced the last of the Committees, on abolition of dual control in 1948, that the earlier reforms were enacted at the pace of the slowest. Had the then Councils (unpaid, by the way) anticipated what was to follow by cutting more ground, as it were, from under the feet of potential critics, the blow when it fell might have been suffered less acutely.

Factors for Reform

I referred above to the abolition in 1948 of the dual control of the old London Stock Exchange – namely, a committee of Trustees and Managers responsible for the property, the 'housekeeping' and finances; a parallel Committee for General Purposes, responsible for all matters concerning members and the conduct of their business. These were entirely independent bodies, a clear segregation of responsibilities going back, in its origins, to the deed of settlement of 1802. Add to this that outsiders could be admitted among the Trustees and Managers, and that proprietorship (by way of freely transferable equity) lay in the hands of some, but not all members, and it is easy to see that later administrators on both sides faced a problem in conflicting loyalties. To this extent it would have been difficult, if not impossible, to reach agreement on rebuilding, let alone such a radical upheaval as necessitated by Big Bang internationalism, had we not moved then to an overall Council. Elderly members spoke heatedly then about the danger of selling their birthright, but strangely, when it came to the ballot-box, seem themselves to have done just that. As usual with the Stock Exchange, it was a matter of voting through the pocket; whatever happened, it was sensed that more would be made by going along with the manoeuvrings. As things were to turn out, they sensed correctly.

So, on the time-scale, this unification of stock market control, by way of a single internal authority, was a vital first stepping stone to change. For the second, many will claim one need only retreat as far as 1978, and more pointedly. Then Shirley Williams, Labour's Secretary of State for Prices and Consumer Affairs, spread the net of the Restrictive Practices Act to cover servicers as well as manufacturers. Acknowledging the odium visited by the Left on the élitist, clublike Stock Exchange, it was not hard to guess at what target this amendment was particularly aimed.

Mantle of Socialism

What was totally unexpected, however, was that the succeeding Tory administration, the 'rich-man's-friend', should have so enthusiastically adopted the mantle of Socialism on their return to power in 1979. Cecil Parkinson, then serving, very briefly, as Secretary of State for Trade, occupied the ground prepared by Mrs Williams and set about putting through the same objective of 'restructuring' the Stock Exchange and all attendant channels of 'popular savings' into the bargain. There could be no piecemeal now.

The object of the Conservative Government, in liberalising (they might have dignified it as liberating) the Stock Exchange was not motivated by the other side's spite and envy, shackles for shackles' sake. There was, as I suspect, a hidden Tory trick that made them jump on the passing bandwagon with indecent haste. It was the fact that their inherited economy had been in serious recession. Although it was hoped that North Sea oil revenue would stop the trade gap (a hope finally denied), the new Government, prompted on by the always avid merchant banks, set its sights high on a growing supplementary input by way of invisible exports. With British manufacturing steadily losing competitiveness in the old, old, throw-away money climate, servicing, in its multiple, transient forms, was seen as an offset to waning visible exports. To achieve this, corporate financiers and multinationalists had to be lured in, and a hugely more profitable, efficient and competitive market established in the strategically well-placed City of London. As Norman Tebbit once perceived ... open during the tail-end of dealings in the Far East and at the beginning of dealings in the United States. The best of both worlds. Of course, the old Stock Exchange, membered by its fliers of paper darts, was none of these things, and had to pull its socks up – or else. In particular, vastly more capital had to be attracted here in order that our competitors could be tackled on the world scene.

The next stepping stone to this end was the lifting of all remaining exchange controls. And this, significantly, was among the first acts of the Thatcherite régime, in October 1979. These controls had been on, in various forms, with their effectiveness changing over time, for more than forty years. They were a great disincentive to our financial competitiveness, hampering outward portfolio investment. It was implicit now, on what was afoot (as I personally believe) in financial servicing, that the inflow of worldwide capital would come only on the assurance of easy and certain repatriation. So, again on a phased time-scale, out of the window went the controls, whatever the consequences in a further appreciation in the exchange rate.

Although it was claimed ostensibly that it was the greater part of the Rule Book which was in contention, most observers (I among them) pin-pointed the Minimum Commission Scale (stockbrokers could charge more, not less) as the cornerstone of change. This was an impediment to competition which it was the Office of Fair Trading's statutory duty to detect and remedy. The overseas would-be participants, notably the world banks, would not subscribe other than to negotiable commission rates, so that, on the now more compacted timetable for dismantlement, the deadline of December 1986 was given for the abolition of fixed commissions. In fact, the then Council saw no point in further torturous delay, and wisely put in the knife for final severance from the past two months ahead. If you sought perversely to rip the engine out of a Rolls Royce and fling it in the ditch, and then wonder why it wouldn't go . . . well, that was the extent of the resounding Bang!

'Fixed Commissions and Jobbers – OUT!'

Together with commissions, everything else fixed – or looking to be 'fixed' – had to be abolished. And this meant the old single capacity – specific jobber and broker (middle-man-principal and agent-dealer for the public) – looked on by intending competitors as a parasite cutting a first slice of the cake, had equally to go. Fixed commissions and the jobbing system could only co-exist in parallel. The newcomers did not understand this intermediary function of the jobber, were unequipped to participate, and so they combined to outlaw the abnormality in favour of dual capacity, Chinese Walls, and more flagrant dishonesty than we had ever known before.

As will now be recognised, the five years 1981-6 saw the full exposure, gradual implementation, and final endorsement of the long-laid plans for the Square Mile – for the intended simplification and ease of dealing; and, more than that, for the protection of the individual investor.

For its initial obduracy over being virtually slaughtered at the post, the Stock Exchange was on the brink of being taken before the Restrictive Practices Court, the judicial arm of the Office of Fair Trading. But the Government saw that a protracted wrangle would impair its invisible earnings, and possibly delay the entry of institutions, at home and abroad, waiting on the sidelines to hugely augment them. And time was running out. As a result a hasty compromise was reached between

Cecil Parkinson and Sir Nicholas Goodison, whereby the OFT dropped its court case against the Stock Exchange, by way of amending legislation in 1982, leaving the latter to proceed on a do-it-yourself basis. This imposed a timetable for dismantlement and restructuring covering roughly three-and-a-half years, to, as already pointed out, a deadline of end-December 1986.

To comprehend the direct reason why the old Stock Exchange was proscribed by the Tory Government, it is necessary, first, to grasp that the monitor of restrictive practice was the OFT, backed for the enforcement of its orders by the Restrictive Practices Court. 'Competition' was the OFT's watchword, and so long a servicers were fully competitive, so went the argument, charges would automatically be constrained, as customers (clients) would, as indeed they were enjoined, 'shop around' for the bargain facilities. But in investment, as in so many other directions, the cheapest is not necessarily the best.

Competition, Choice and Cheap Dealing ... Oh!

The ironical point of all this is that in the end, with its high-profile Big Bang, this Government may have done precisely the opposite to what it intended: destroyed the bulwarks protecting the small investor; made the loudly proclaimed 'popular investment' infinitely more expensive, not to say difficult; and impaired the level of invisible exports because the initially enchanted internationalists are now thoroughly disenchanted with the London mirage. They are here now not so much for what they can reasonably contribute, but for what they can pillage from our fine, viable, expanding industrial concerns by way of manipulative takeovers, whether or not these eventually materialise or as the means of a quick rake-off.

[136]

When it comes specifically to protecting the individual investor, who was not really on equal terms with the institutional investor, single capacity was always seen, however grudgingly, as the best method, if you mean avoidance of purposeful leaks. As to competition, nothing gave a wider choice than the old jobbing system, with its great diversity of practitioners all making variants of the same price basis. If, indeed, *choice* is the DTI's aim, as allegedly it is, the customer in the saloon bar has nothing like the same choice as formerly provided the investor: perhaps a dozen different jobbers in Dunlops. But then the brewing industry is a vast revenue-producer, and, as such, sacrosanct.

The very reason why the early share dealers came into such ill-repute was because they were engaged in a variety of activities – say, bookselling in the morning, broking-cum-jobbing of an afternoon – dual capacity in the absolute. It was this conflict of interest that had gradually to be worked out of the system throughout the last century. Now it has been officially reinstated.

With fixed commissions, the vital protection here lay in the fact that stockbrokers could not competitively undercut each other for business. Oh, dear! this was a real denial of the sought-after competition. Yet exploiters are never content with the happy medium. This was the experience immediately after Big Bang. Many of the new conglomerates lost immense sums, and other smaller firms were structurally weakened to the detriment of everybody by offering cheaper services in an attempt to grab a market share. This policy was quickly reversed, and now the swing of the pendulum is violently the other way, putting the small investor out into the cold. The ultimate irony is that those who conceived the whole policy have no way of retrieving the position for the new, bank-encumbered market. Or if anybody has, they are remarkably quiet about it.

Well, well ...

To whatever distance the observer chooses to retreat in contemplation of the origins of Big Bang, to whatever causes and contentions you may attribute that venture, most reflective writers seem now to regard it as hasty, ill-conceived, and a capitulation to the world banks. But the immediate reception by the Press of the first outlining of the proposals seemed to me to be ecstatic. No stone was turned, no twig stirred, in the way of investigative journalism. Few commentators apparently looked for, or could sensibly visualise, any snags in the proposals. But then the financial Press was always critical of the seclusive attitude of the Stock Exchange membership. We were looked on largely as public-schoolboys which, in fact, was far from numerically the truth. But the editors were sufficiently awake, at the same time, to the prospect of financial advertising on a scale to mute criticism of any quarter; the not unnatural urge was to let the whole business off the hook and wind it up for as far as the column inches would take it.

And so they did.

Well, well ... we'll see?

GLOSSARY

Account   The Stock Exchange divides the year into twenty-four two- or three-week periods called Accounts. Settlement of accounts, payable or receivable, is effected within six business days following the end of the fortnightly Account, on the seventh day with the three-weeker, except for cash settlement transactions (e.g. gilts). Completion of a matching buying or selling transaction (or vice versa) within the same Account period attracts only one commission, that on 'Closing' being free. But Stamp Duty is now payable (0.5%). On these 'Closing' trades the balance of difference in buying and selling is payable on Settlement day.

Alpha   The roughly 140 top quality shares (often termed 'blue chips') officially quoted on the International Stock Exchange. The descending categories then by degree of the freedom of dealing designated – Beta, Gamma, Delta.

Application form   Securities offered for public subscription require application to be made on a special form, obtainable from the issuing house or from the company's brokers or bankers.

Asset value   The asset value per ordinary share is derived from the net current assets, plus estimated value of fixed assets, divided by the number of shares in issue.

Bargain   Colloquialism for the deal/trade between practitioners in the stock market. Derives from the earlier physical bargaining between stockbroker and stockjobber on the old Stock Exchange. Does not imply value or inevitable profit.

Base rate   Former Bank Rate. Determined by the High Street banks in conjunction with the Bank of England. Indicates cost of money and is the rate to which all other lenders and borrowers broadly conform.

Bear   Opposite of the 'bull' described below. One who is pessimistic of the prospects and acts accordingly.

Big Bang   Implemented on 27 October 1986. The Tory Government's insisted reorganisation of the 200-year-old Stock Exchange under the control of the banks (high street and merchant), together with the admission of international bankers, brokers and fund operators on a worldwide scale. Result: the International Stock Exchange under the indirect control of the Securities Investment Board (SIB), a central agency accountable to Parliament, but as with all other financial servicers, under the direct control of its own Self-Regulating Organisation (SRO). This last is abbreviated TSA (The Securities Association).

Boom   The long upward market cycle carried to extremity.

Bull   An operator/investor persuaded that the stock/share of his choice is going up in price. The stock market may be described as 'bullish' when most are of the same persuasion.

[140]

Capitalisation issue	Issue to existing shareholders of new shares credited as fully-paid by way of a capitalisation of reserves and allotted free of charge in proportion to existing holdings. Sometimes termed 'free share bonus'. The share price is automatically adjusted proportionately.
Chartism	The technique of the chartist described below.
Chartists	Once described by Jim Slater as men with long overdrafts and dirty raincoats, these are the students and exponents of chartism – the interpretation of charts, graphs, and indices, in attempted judgement on future trends. Part of the whole technical analysis which endeavours to indicate *when* the investor should act, as distinct from *in what* the investor should act.
Chinese Walls	The intangible division between the corporate finance/analytical and the investment management departments of financial institutions to prevent the misuse of inside information privy to the first by the second. The share dealer must not in any way be influenced by, or personally take advantage of, price sensitive information. To do so is to border dangerously on the area of 'insider' trading.
Dividend cover	The number of times the cost of the annual dividend is provided by the net profit.
Dual capacity	The post-Big Bang abandonment of the old-style single capacity system unique to London (distinctive jobber and broker – principal and agent) in favour of a dealer acting in both capacities. Hence the now dubious Chinese Walls to keep instinctively enveigling youngsters apart.
Equities	Equity – equality of treatment, impartiality. Another description for ordinary shares representative of a company's risk capital with

entitlement to all the distributable benefits after meeting all interest obligations on prior charge capital. Ordinary/equity shares carry the crucial voting rights.

Fundamental analysis

As described under 'Chartists', the fundamentalist is concerned with *in what* to invest, on a critical assessment of the fundamentals of the business correlated from past figures and result.

Gearing

The ratio between loan capital, preference capital, and ordinary capital. High gearing means that the prior and fixed-interest charges are high in proportion to the ordinary capital. The ordinary shares are consequently sensitive to changes of fortune. Low gearing is the reverse.

Grossing-up

With reference here to dividend payments and income return: adding back the deducted tax to the net figure in order to obtain the gross figure.

Insider

An investment practitioner/adviser/dealer working from, engaged within, the City circle; supposedly in receipt of, or capable of having access to, confidential ('inside') information.

Kerb-crawlers

Speculators who formerly attended in Throgmorton Street, literally inhabiting the kerbs and dealing there with their half-commission in earnest attendance.

Leak

The injudicious imparting of private, inside, possibly extremely price-sensitive information, therefore said to be 'leaked'. Often grossly distorted by repeated rumour-mongering.

Marketability

The degree of freedom or otherwise in dealing in a particular share. The unmarketable (sometimes termed illiquid) securities are largely in the delta category.

Nominal value

Equally par value. Representing the nominal amount of capital issued up by a company on its public promotion, and as subsequently increased. If a company initially issues £100,000 of ordinary stock corresponding with £100,000 of its Authorised capital, such could be traded in stock-units basically valued at £1, 50p, 25p, or any convenient multiple of £1. Nowadays there are usually 25p shares/units, and unless stated to the contrary in the price columns, this is the assumption. It does not matter in what unit the publicly quoted capital is represented – for example, one million 10p shares to the £100,000 – provided each has a uniform nominal value.

P/E

Price-earnings ratio, which is the current share price divided by the earnings per share in pence.

Pre-tax profit

The amount retained by a company after deducting operating costs and adjusting for other income such as interest on investments and non-trading sources.

Primary cycle

Term used in chartism to denote the long overall graph line from bottom to top (or the reverse), largely ignoring intermediate fluctuations.

Privatisation

The Government's conversion of publicly owned minerals, supply and essential services back into private hands by way of vast capital flotations. The distinguishing feature of the stock market during 1986 and '87.

Rights issue

Additional permanent capital raised by the offer for cash of new shares to existing holders, in proportion to their holdings and at a preferential price. Issued by way of a provisional allotment letter which is negotiable and may be renounced in favour of a purchaser should the new shares go to a premium over the issue price and the allottee desire to secure a profit.

SEAQ   Abbreviation for Stock Exchange Automatic Quotations system.

'Sideways'   In sluggish markets, shares going nowhere slowly, often described as moving 'sideways'.

Third market   Instigated by the Stock Exchange in January 1987, to encourage entry by companies too small to qualify for the USM (Unlisted Securities Market).

Trading profit Annual amount retained by a company after deducting operating costs from the value of sales.

Watered   When a company's assets value per ordinary share is diluted (reduced) by a new issue of capital without a corresponding increase in assets.

Yield   The annual income return offered by a security in gross percentage terms. Explained in Chapter 7, 'Yardsticks of Value'.

INDEX